Windows 8 for the Older and Wiser

Get Up and Running on Your Computer

Adrian Arnold and Richard Millett

WILEY

A John Wiley and Sons, Ltd, Publication

ISBN 978-1-119-94155-2 (paperback); ISBN 978-1-119-94360-0 (epdf); ISBN 978-1-119-94361-7 (epub); ISBN 978-1-119-94362-4 (emobi)

A catalogue record for this book is available from the British Library.

Set in 11/13 Optima LT Std by Linotype, Bad Homburg, Germany

Printed in the U.K. at Bell & Bain

Dedication

To my wonderful family.
— Adrian Arnold

The Third Age Trust

The Third Age Trust is the body which represents all U3As in the UK. The U3A movement is made up of over 700 self-governing groups of older men and women who organise for themselves activities which may be educational, recreational or social in kind. Calling on their own experience and knowledge they demand no qualifications nor do they offer any. The movement has grown at a remarkable pace and offers opportunities to thousands of people to demonstrate their own worth to one another and to the community. Their interests are astonishingly varied but the members all value the opportunity to share experiences and learning with like-minded people. The Third Age Trust's endorsement of the Older and Wiser series hints at some of that width of interest.

THE THIRD AGE TRUST

THE UNIVERSITY OF THE THIRD AGE

Contents

Introduction — 1

Age considerations — 2

Stretching the mind — 3

Guardian angels — 3

Uses of a home computer — 3

Using the Internet — 4

Beginners' fears — 6

Equipment needed — 8

How to use this book — 12

Part I – Learning the Basics — 15

Chapter 1 – Getting started — 17

About Windows 8 — 17

Turning the computer on — 18

The Start screen and Desktop screen 19

Apps and applications 21

Controlling the computer 22

Turning the computer off 33

Chapter 2 – Using the Start screen   37

The Lock screen 37

The Start menu 38

Tiles 39

Opening and closing apps 41

Charms 43

Searching the computer 47

Chapter 3 – Using the Desktop interface   51

Icons 53

Taskbar 54

Organising the Desktop 56

Multitasking 59

Chapter 4 – Using windows   63

The structure of a window 64

Title bar 64

Ribbon tabs 66

Toolbar ribbon 67

Breadcrumb bar 67

Side bar 68

Opening a window 69

The main window 70

Part II – Digging Deeper   73

Chapter 5 – Navigating the system   75

Disks, drives and memory 75

Memory 76

Libraries 77

Folders 78

Files 80

Chapter 6 – Customising the computer   89

The Settings menu 89

Control Panel 95

Power settings 96

Searching the computer for apps, settings and files 96

Changing the pointer settings 98

Chapter 7 – Opening your first app ⬤ 101

The Solitaire app	102
The Paint app	104
The Maps app	108
Searching Maps	111
Menus	112
Moving between apps	112

Chapter 8 – Opening your first Desktop application ⬤ 115

Opening an application	115
Selecting text	117
Formatting text	118
Dropdown menus	120
Further selection tips	121
Deleting text	122
Inserting text	122
The Quick Access bar	122
The Undo and Redo icons	124
The Backspace and Delete keys	124
Saving your work	125
Finding files	128

Chapter 9 – Getting help · 131

Help menus · 132
Windows Help facility · 133
Getting help from the Internet · 135
Hung programs · 135
Task Manager · 135
Keyboard shortcuts · 137
Last resort · 138

Part III – Connecting and Protecting · 141

Chapter 10 – Connecting to the Internet · 143

How the Internet works · 143
Internet Service Providers (ISPs) · 145
Choosing an ISP · 146
Broadband · 147
Internet costs · 148
Setting up your Internet connection · 149
Payment · 151

Chapter 11 – Protecting yourself online · 155

What is security? · 155
Malware · 156

Contents

Financial transactions   159
Personal records   162
Backing up   162
Wi-Fi security   165

Chapter 12 – Using email   **171**

The concept of email   171
Windows 8 email   172
Desktop mail   182

Chapter 13 – Using the Internet   **189**

Desktop Internet Explorer   190
Setting your own Home Page   195
Internet Explorer   196

Part IV – Having Fun   **203**

Chapter 14 – Exploring Windows apps **205**

About the Windows Store   205
Downloading an app   209
Removing/unpinning an app   212
Using apps   213
Viewing contacts   215

Moving between apps   217

PCWisdom   219

Chapter 15 – Installing software   **223**

Installing a program from a disc   223

Chapter 16 – Search engines   **237**

Google   238

Alternative search engines   247

Chapter 17 – Shopping online   **251**

Economics of the web   251

Financial security   252

A practice purchase   253

Registering with a website   257

Completing your purchase   257

Chapter 18 – Booking travel online   **261**

Ticketless booking   262

Booking a flight with EasyJet   262

Low-fare advertisements   266

Booking train and coach travel   266

Contents

Chapter 19 – Entertainment   273

Playing CDs and DVDs   274

Ripping music   275

Playing DVDs   276

Windows 8 Music app   276

Spotify   278

Listening to the radio on the computer   280

TV players   280

Movies on the computer   281

Slide shows   282

Chapter 20 – Introducing social networking   287

Using Facebook   288

Glossary   293

Index   297

Acknowledgments

This book would never have been completed were it not for the stimulation, support and encouragement I have received from many people but a number of them deserve specific recognition.

Richard Millett has been a tower of strength with his detailed knowledge of Windows operating systems. We have been supported by several members of the Wiley publishing house but I would like to mention four people in particular. Birgit Gruber who has overseen the project with much-needed encouragement during some dark hours; Ellie Scott who has handled the small but essential technical issues in such a cheerful manner and finally our two editors, Grace Fairley and Beth Taylor, who have tidied up the manuscript in such a thoughtful way. Finally, I could not have written this book without the limitless support and encourage from my wife, Jen. My heartfelt thanks go to you all.

— Adrian Arnold

About the Authors

Adrian Arnold qualified as a veterinary surgeon from Cambridge University in 1964. He set up his own general practice in Crawley in 1968. Having created a four-man, two centre practice the family decided to move to Colchester in Essex where he set up another new practice in 1987. Throughout this time he became a freelance journalist contributing to the national, local and veterinary press. In 1989 he became one of the first vets in the country to computerise his veterinary records and computing has remained his hobby ever since.

For the past 20 years, he has enjoyed teaching members of the older generation how to use their home computers both privately as well as acting as a tutor for AgeUK and the University of the Third Age (U3A).

His other hobbies have included light aircraft flying, digital photography and travelling to meet friends and relatives in Europe, America, Africa and Asia.

Adrian and his wife, Jen, who has just retired after 21 years as a magistrate, have three children and four grandchildren. They are about to move from Essex to Somerset to be closer to their family.

Richard Millett is a lead instructor working for Firebrand Training. He has over 30 years experience in the computer industry and has worked with all versions of Windows since its inception. He is responsible for producing training material for companies, specialising in Computer Security. He also delivers training courses over a wide range of computing topics to all ages ranging from young apprentices to groups from the Third Age. He currently lives in Berkshire with his wife Shelagh and two cats.

Publisher's Acknowledgements

Some of the people who helped bring this book to market include the following:

Editorial and Production
VP Consumer and Technology Publishing Director: Michelle Leete
Associate Director–Book Content Management: Martin Tribe
Associate Publisher: Chris Webb
Senior Commissioning Editor: Birgit Gruber
Assistant Editor: Ellie Scott
Development Editors: Grace Fairley, Beth Taylor
Copy Editors: Grace Fairley, Beth Taylor
Editorial Manager: Jodi Jensen
Senior Project Editor: Sara Shlaer
Editorial Assistant: Leslie Saxman

Marketing
Associate Marketing Director: Louise Breinholt
Marketing Manager: Lorna Mein
Senior Marketing Executive: Kate Parrett

Composition Services
Compositors: Lissa Auciello-Brogan, Carrie Cesavice, Jennifer Henry
Proofreader: Tricia Liebig
Indexer: Potomac Indexing, LLC

Icons used in this book

Throughout this book, we've used icons to help focus your attention on certain information. This is what they mean:

 Equipment needed — Lets you know in advance the equipment you will need to hand as you progress through the chapter.

 Skills needed — Placed at the beginning to help identify the skills you'll need for the chapter ahead.

 Tip — Tips and suggestions to help make life easier.

 Note — Take note of these little extras to avoid confusion.

 Warning — Read carefully; a few things could go wrong at this point.

 Try It — Go on, enjoy yourself; you won't break it.

 Trivia — A little bit of fun to bring a smile to your face.

 Summary — A short recap at the end of each chapter.

 Brain Training — Test what you've learned from the chapter.

PRACTICE MAKES PERFECT

To build upon the lessons learnt in this book, visit www.pcwisdom.co.uk

- **More training tutorials**

- **Links to resources**

- **Advice through frequently asked questions**

- **Social networking tips**

- **Videos and podcasts from the author**

- **Author blogs**

Introduction

This book is written for those of a certain age who are about to use a computer for the first time, as well as those who are already familiar with earlier editions of the Windows operating systems such as XP, Vista and Windows 7. You have our word that there are very few acronyms and those that do appear will be fully explained in the text. We assume you have no previous computing knowledge, experience or keyboard skills, while technical jargon will be noticeable only by its complete absence.

The book is written in plain, understandable English. We could describe Windows 8 as "an operating system capable of using both 32- and 64-bit technology, which is far less power hungry than its predecessors". This would only scare the living daylights out of you and make you quickly return the book to the bookshelf, determined to go back to your familiar pastimes of bridge, gardening or cookery. Instead, we will tell you that Windows 8 is just a new way of getting your computer to do what you want. You do not have to understand computer technology any more than you have to understand the mechanics of the fuel injection system in order to drive your car.

This book is aimed solely at people who use personal computers (PCs), using the latest Windows 8 system. Apple Mac computers work in a very different way, so I'm afraid we are unable to cater to Mac users in this book. Users of previous Windows operating systems will find Windows 8 quite a steep learning curve. This book will act as an escalator to ease the climb. If you are completely new to computers, you will be at an advantage at this stage because you will have no previous preconceptions of how a computer should be operated.

The first few chapters take you gently through the basic skills of turning the machine on and off, the appearance and function of the computer screen and the basic use of the keyboard, mouse, trackpad and touchscreen. You are then introduced to the easier functions of a computer, such as typing a letter, sending a message and exploring the Internet. At this point, complete beginners will be asking, "What is a trackpad?" You might recognise that a touchscreen sounds as if it might be like an interactive television screen and you will have heard of the Internet — but you might have no idea of what they are or how they work. Have no fear, all will be explained in words you can understand, using everyday activities as examples such as driving a car, operating a washing machine and using a cash machine. You might not be aware of it, but all of these use computers too.

Age considerations

You may be nervous about taking up computing, having watched younger members of your family typing at lightning speed while unintelligible words and images flash across the computer screen. You may even have seen someone open up the computer case to carry out a minor repair, revealing a forest of cables, cityscapes of tiny plastic squares and the Egyptian hieroglyphics of circuit boards. You do not have to have this sort of knowledge of the workings of a computer any more than you have to be able to rewire a telephone exchange to make a phone call or replace the cam belt of your car in order to drive it. In our 20 years of teaching, we have had the pleasure of teaching more than 20 90-year-olds, two of whom have now developed their own websites, which they continue to maintain.

As we get older, our minds may be a little slower and our memory less reliable but if you are fortunate enough to have retained sufficient faculties to drive a car or use a washing machine you will have little difficulty in following the instructions given in this book. If you can set your television to record a programme you are eligible for Class 3, nevermind the beginners class.

Our joints may become stiffer and our eyes may need glasses as we get older but we gain compensating advantages such as experience and, above all, we have more time. Our offspring rarely have the benefit of such a luxury while they are juggling work, home life and school runs. This book allows you to set your own learning pace. There is no exam deadline. Consider the fact that if you make a driving mistake, you may land up in a hospital but, if you make a mistake on the computer, you can always switch it off and put the kettle on.

Some familiarity with a typewriter keyboard is an advantage but not a necessity. We have been computing for more than 35 years and still only use about four fingers. You may find it frustrating to 'hunt and peck' for the correct keys when you begin but familiarity and speed come with practice.

Stretching the mind

So what do you need to be able to use a computer? Apart from the computer itself, two essentials are enthusiasm and a desire to learn. Computers are not essential to a happy, fulfilling life. Your time might already be filled with committee meetings, golf rounds, bridge clubs, gardening and frequent caravan holidays. But if you have the time and enthusiasm to expand your knowledge of anything from ancient civilizations to the care of orchids, then the Internet is your oyster, offering a limitless reference library and access to all sorts of activities. Above all, it should be fun.

Guardian angels

These people are invaluable. They may be neighbours, friends or relatives. They might be 16 or 60 but they have been around the computing world for some while. They do not have to have a degree in computer science. They are not there to 'teach' you so much as to help you buy the right computer, set up your system so that it works properly and put it right when things go wrong.

Guardian angels are worth their weight in gold but are usually very happy to accept remuneration in the form of a cup of tea, a glass of wine or an offer to babysit. We will be referring to these divine helpers throughout the book.

Uses of a home computer

With a basic computer, you can keep a diary, write letters, create posters, catalogue your CD collection and maintain financial records and membership lists. You can remove the dreaded 'red eye' from digital photographs, sharpen and straighten images and even remove telegraph poles sprouting from people's heads. The computer will also play your favourite music tracks while you are performing any of these tasks.

And that's before you consider the wealth of possibilities that open up to you with access to the Internet, which we cover in the next section.

If all this sounds daunting, fear not. In this book, we will begin to scratch the surface of what is possible. By the time you have finished it, you will have gained the necessary basic skills to continue your explorations into digital photography, family history, social networking and the advanced use of word processing, spreadsheet, database and presentation programs — all of which are covered in greater depth by other books in the *Older and Wiser* series.

Using the Internet

The Internet is essentially a vast network of computers linked by cable, satellite and wireless connections forming a spider's web that spans the world. These machines vary in size from the humblest home computer to huge computer banks, called 'servers', housed in air-conditioned office blocks. The World Wide Web, or 'web' for short, refers to this network, which allows you to access information stored in these enormous computers. The concept of the Internet is explained in Chapter 10, and we explain how to use it in Chapter 13.

A computer linked to the outside world via the Internet expands your horizons to a whole new world. It allows you to maintain communication with friends and relatives across the globe. You can even enjoy free video conversations with people on other continents. It provides you with dictionaries, atlases, libraries, teaching manuals, a vast encyclopaedia and a wealth of other information, and you can send people photographs and documents in seconds instead of using the traditional post. It can translate your words into foreign languages, or allow you to watch video tutorials on painting and drawing, DIY projects, gardening and a vast range of esoteric hobbies — in fact, you'll find information on every subject under the sun on the Internet. You can listen to the radio and watch repeats of your favourite TV programmes, and you'll find that researching your family tree is much easier on the Internet. The possibilities of using an Internet-linked home computer are almost endless.

Communication

Research has shown that the most popular function of the home computer is email. This is a form of instant communication between two or more computers. You simply type your message, enter the recipient's address, perhaps attach a photo or other document, and click on the Send button. Within seconds, your message is delivered to the addressee's mailbox, where they will collect it the next time they check their mailbox. We explain how to use email in Chapter 12.

Information

Today's parents often lead such frenetic lives that they have little time to sit down with their offspring; however, when grandparents have basic computing skills they can communicate with the youngsters on their own terms while taking the opportunity to pass on their life experiences at the same time. While we are not suggesting that we can be of much help if our grandchildren are studying advanced mathematical theory, we can help them with their research into things like the history of the Second World War, while adding our personal experiences of that time. If we need to, we can get the full facts about things we might be worried about (like solvent abuse, for example) as well as learn enough about modern culture to discuss the merits or otherwise of the latest *X Factor* winner.

Such information on the web is, in most cases, completely free. You may have to register your name and address to get the full benefit from some websites but such subscriptions rarely incur a fee. There are a few websites that charge for membership but these are currently often academic or financial sites. It's worth noting, however, that increasing numbers of newspapers are beginning to charge small subscription fees to view some or all of their content, or their archives. Chapter 16 deals with how to find information.

Shopping

Buying goods and services from the Internet is the second most common use of the home computer. Internet shopping can result in very significant savings to the household budget. Books and music CDs were among the first items to be sold in any large numbers on the Internet but you can now buy almost anything. Hotel bookings, travel tickets, utility services, insurance and many household goods are much cheaper when bought on the Internet.

You can have your weekly supermarket shop delivered to your door, avoiding the need to carry heavy items home from the store, saving on petrol and parking fees and stipulating the time of day you want your order to be delivered. Internet shopping is covered in Chapter 17.

Hobbies

You may have an urge to take up carpentry, a foreign language, ballroom dancing or tai chi. No matter what your interest or enthusiasm, you will find information and tutorials on the Internet — even how to construct a 3D origami swan. Many tutorials are available in the form of video lessons. For instance, it would be difficult to write a lesson on how to correct your sliced tennis serve but a video can explain the technique very easily. Gardeners will find a wealth of information on the Internet. There are more than two million web pages devoted to the pruning of roses.

Sports

Every sport devised by man can be researched on the Internet. If you feel the need to view the scorecard of the second Test match against the Australians at Lords in 1993, you only have to click on a few links to get the information. Facts about the Beijing Olympics are easily available, together with the latest women's lacrosse match between the North Carolina Tar Heels and the Northwestern Wildcats! Anyone know the rules of pelota?

Travel

How far is it from the centre of Paris to a village just north of Frankfurt? How long would it take to drive by car? No problem. The Internet will supply the answers. Fancy a weekend break in the Scottish Highlands? Booking travel on the Internet can result in significant savings. What did previous guests think of a particular hotel? All these answers and many more are waiting just around the computer corner. Booking travel on the Internet is covered in Chapter 18.

Beginners' fears

One of the main objectives we had in mind when writing this book was to allay, or at least reduce, the fears that many beginners experience when considering the use of a computer for the first time. There are many such fears, but three of them stand out for all beginners: the fear of breaking the machine, the fear of losing everything on the computer and the very human fear of looking stupid. There is also a fourth fear, which is mainly applicable to men.

Fear of breaking the computer

For all their electronic intricacy, computers are remarkably tolerant of abuse. Spilling coffee on a laptop will severely damage the computer — but it would have the same effect on a television set. Resting a heavy book on the keyboard may cause the screen to flicker and display strange menus, but this is easily rectified without recourse to major repair. Common sense in the use of the computer will avoid any lasting damage to the machine. We have all been using cameras for many years without dropping them onto hard surfaces or immersing them in water. The same care should be taken with computers.

We are not saying that computers don't go wrong — they can do, but at this stage it is unlikely to be your fault. Cars occasionally grind to a halt in the fast lane of the motorway, for instance, but they are the exception to the rule.

Fear of losing all your work

This worry is much more understandable. You will probably find that your first news-laden email to your Australian cousin takes the best part of an hour to compose, pecking at the keys with a couple of fingers; the last thing you need is then to lose all your hard work. Fortunately, the computer can often prevent this kind of disaster by reminding you to save your work when you have finished. If you make sure to save your documents regularly as you are working on them, the most likely cause of losing your work will be a failure of the power supply and even then you may find that the computer has been quietly saving your work in the background so that you will only lose the last few minutes of work before the power failed. It is really quite difficult to erase all information from a computer but it is prudent to save your precious files onto an external hard disc at weekly intervals. We will discuss this and other security measures in Chapter 11.

Fear of looking stupid

Embarrassment is a peculiarly human emotion. We can all sometimes feel that everyone else knows the answers to the silly questions that keep nagging us. They don't. They would just prefer to remain ignorant rather than appear 'stupid'. We all make mistakes throughout our lives — they are the tools of learning. Using this book will allow you to hide yourself away from superior prying eyes, make mistakes, laugh at yourself and try again. You will inevitably come across well-meaning friends and relatives who offer to show you how to do something on the computer. Watch what they do, but do not feel the need to learn from them. 'Teaching' and 'showing' are completely different techniques.

Fear of accidentally accessing pornography

Several of my pupils, usually men, have expressed a real fear that had never previously occurred to us — that of accidentally accessing pornographic websites. This is a sad fear, which reflects badly on our times. Forensic computer scientists can extract the smallest details of your web browsing activity. It is perfectly possible that you may access an unsuitable site inadvertently. For instance, you may be researching some facts about the Knights of the Round Table but mistakenly enter an incorrect search phrase such as 'Nights of the Round Table', which brings up pornographic material. Don't feel bad when such an incident happens. Your computer is not going to shine a red light on your head to advertise your shame! The authorities recognise that such errors occur.

Financial security on the Internet

The majority of our students have a natural anxiety about revealing details of their bank accounts and credit cards to the criminal element lurking on the Internet. It seems as though we read about identity theft in the media every other day — but we also read about fatal train accidents and they rarely prevent us from travelling by rail. Let's face it, we are probably in more danger of losing our credit cards by leaving our purse or wallet on a shop counter than having our encrypted financial transactions intercepted on the Internet. Chapter 11 deals extensively with computer and Internet security.

Equipment needed

Let us assume that you have taken the plunge and bought a computer. What sort of computer will you need? How much RAM will you need? Should you go for a 2.33 megahertz chip or opt for a faster 2.7 MHz machine? How big is a 500 gigabyte hard disk?

And you thought we were going to avoid technical language in this book! You probably don't understand any of these questions, let alone know how to answer them effectively. This is where your guardian angel comes in. He or she will be able to translate this esoteric jargon into words of one or two syllables and advise you about the most suitable machine for your needs.

There are, however, a number of decisions that you need to make before visiting the store.

What type of computer should you get?

In recent years, computers have developed into many different varieties. These include desktop computers, laptops and tablet computers:

● **Desktop computers** take up a lot of room and require separate monitor screen, keyboard, mouse, web cameras and microphones, many of which require different cable connections. They tend to offer more for your money, larger screens and the opportunity to upgrade the machine at a later date.

● **Laptops** incorporate the computer, monitor screen and keyboard. They take up less room and can be used anywhere, not just a particular place in the house. Laptops can operate in both battery and mains power mode, which means you may not need to be close to a power point. Laptop batteries last a lot longer than they used to — they usually give you about six hours of reasonable use but there is nothing more frustrating than a battery that suddenly dies on you. Laptops also have a smaller cousin called the netbook. This has similar functionality as a laptop but is physically smaller.

● **Tablets** are very small computers that dispense with the keyboard. They usually have touchscreens for viewing photographs, documents and web pages, and display a 'virtual' keyboard on the screen to enable typing.

Microsoft has just launched a new tablet computer, named Surface, which is designed to make the best use of the Windows 8 system. It will come with a magnetic cover that incorporates a keyboard and trackpad. Initially there will be two versions with different amounts of permanent memory. It is launched to challenge the success of the Apple iPad.

The iPad is currently the most popular tablet computer but it does not use Windows 8 technology. Many more Windows-compatible tablet computers will become available following the launch of Windows 8.

If you have a designated study or an available spare bedroom, then a desktop with its larger screen and its cables tidied away may be the best option. If you are restricted for space and only have a kitchen table to work on, a laptop or netbook would be more suitable. We have noticed a significant shift from the desktop to the laptop over the past five years.

You will need a number of power sockets, even with a laptop, but an extension unit with four power points will be more than adequate. To use the Internet, you will also need access to a telephone socket. Some desktop machines need to be connected by a cable to access the Internet so will need to be close to a telephone point. Laptops usually receive their signal wirelessly from a remote box called a modem router, which plugs into the telephone socket anywhere in the home.

Do you need a printer?

You will need a printer to print out tickets, recipes, emails and the occasional photo. A printer will take up quite a lot of space but it does not have to be permanently plugged in to the computer. If you intend to use a laptop in the kitchen or at a small desk, you can always keep the printer elsewhere and attach the computer only when you need to print out a document.

How will you connect to the Internet?

Computers can be connected to the telephone system and thence to the Internet in three ways. A *wired connection* is where a cable runs from a socket in the computer to the telephone socket. *Wireless connection, also called Wi-Fi,* requires a box called a modem router plugged into the telephone point, which broadcasts the signal to a receiver built into the computer. Almost all laptops use this method of Internet connection, although they can be wired if necessary. The third method of Internet connection uses *mobile phone technology*. A small device, called a dongle, receives a mobile telephone signal and conveys it to the computer when plugged in. This can be very useful if you intend to use your computer while travelling but the call charges can prove to be expensive.

How much money are you prepared to spend?

A perfectly adequate computer with Windows 8 installed should cost less than £500. You can find pretty good printers (with built-in photocopiers and scanners) for under

£100. Since you are almost certainly going to need access to the Internet, you will have to budget for an Internet subscription of £15 to £20 a month. You can get some good deals if you buy a telephone/TV/Internet package from the same company.

Where should you buy it?

National computer chain stores offer a wider range of options but their support facilities vary from the good to the downright dreadful, and they have a tendency to persuade you to buy more than you need. If there is a fault with the computer they will often return it to the manufacturer for repair — a process that can take as long as four weeks or more. Individual local computer shops should be able to supply you with a machine perfectly suited to your needs. They usually repair faulty machines in-house, often with a 48-hour turnaround, and they are more likely to sell you what you need rather than the latest all-singing, all-dancing, wallet-lightening machine.

What are your minimum specifications?

Now comes the technical bit! For the benefit of your guardian angel, we suggest the following minimum specifications that will cope with everything described in this book — and beyond:

- A 17" desktop screen or 15.4" laptop machine (you can get smaller screens, and they may come cheaper but they can strain your eyes after a while)
- A processor speed of at least 2.3 GHz
- 3 or 4GB of RAM
- A hard disk of at least 500GB
- 2 USB ports
- 1-year warranty
- A wireless modem router (this will reduce the number of wires you can trip over)
- Windows 8 operating system
- We strongly recommend the purchase of a multifunction printer/scanner at an early stage. You will soon feel the need to print out emails, letters, web pages, recipes and tutorials. Many printers now come with wireless communication which avoids further wiring.

Please do not try to understand these guidelines. They are simply included for the benefit of your guardian angel.

How to use this book

This book has been written on a computer using the early versions of Windows 8. The program has now been launched in its final version but there will be alterations, updates and improvements over the initial few months following its launch. Any alterations will be available on the accompanying website at **www.pcwisdom. co.uk** where you can find the very latest information as it arrives. Please use the site to ask Adrian any questions that are not covered by the book. You can also email him with your queries at **bu33kin@live.co.uk**.

You should work through the chapters in the book in sequence. Part I takes you through the very basics of the different types of screen; using the keyboard, mouse, trackpad and touchscreen; and the Windows display modes. Part II then progresses to opening your first program (or 'application') and learning to type a letter on the computer. Windows 8 uses a lot of smaller programs called 'apps' and we will lead you gently through several of the common ones. We also look at getting help. Part III covers email and the Internet, including composing your first email message and how to make best use of the Internet by using web addresses and search engines. In Part IV, you will find out how to use the computer for shopping, booking travel tickets and entertainment. This is followed by a glossary of common computing terms and an index.

This is not to say that the book must be followed slavishly. You may already be fully conversant with the use of the keyboard and mouse, in which case you could skip part of Chapter 1 and concentrate on the new aspects of Windows 8 and the specific skills that you really want to learn.

Windows 8 is the most comprehensive revision of the Windows operating system since the arrival of Windows 95 in 1995. Even if you have had experience of previous Windows operating systems, we strongly recommend that you study Chapters 1, 2 and 3 before assuming that your previous experience will carry you through. Windows 8 uses a Start screen interface, which makes use of touchscreen technology, as well as the more familiar Desktop interface, which normally uses the keyboard and mouse.

One final word of advice. This book is supposed to be fun. You will make mistakes — they are part of the learning process. Don't sit and tear your hair out or beat yourself up when things do not turn out as you expect. Just turn off the computer and do something else for a while — the computer will still be there tomorrow.

Summary

- A computer can open up a whole new world of communication, information and fun.

- Windows 8 is a very different incarnation of the Windows operating system. Those familiar with the older systems will find the new system a very different experience while beginners will have the advantage of gaining computing experience without previous preconceptions.

- Your guardian angel will prove an invaluable lifeline at this stage of your computing career so now is the time to ask the right person if they would mind giving you a bit of help now and again. But don't be a pain in the butt — try and figure things out for yourself and make notes of your problems so that a session with your angel will be as productive as possible without taxing their patience.

- Windows 8 uses two distinct interfaces — Start screen and Desktop. Start screen uses apps while the Desktop operates larger programs (known as applications).

- The important thing is to have fun learning while you gradually gain confidence in using your new computer.

Brain training

There may be more than one correct answer to the questions.

1. What can you do using a home computer?

   a) Conduct video telephone calls free of charge across the world

   b) Find ways to save money on your utility bills

   c) Mow the grass

   d) Watch TV programmes

2. What is a tablet?

   a) A prescription program to repair a computer

   b) A device that connects your computer to the telephone line

   c) A small computer without a physical keyboard

   d) A small reminder note

3. Why do you need a printer?

   a) You don't

   b) A computer will not work unless it is connected to a printer

   c) To print out travel tickets, documents and emails

   d) To be able to use the Internet

4. What is a modem router?

   a) A GPS mapping device used in a car

   b) Another word for an atlas

   c) A device that connects your computer to the Internet via your telephone line

   d) A security device

5. What happens if the battery of your laptop computer runs out?

   a) You will lose all information stored on the laptop

   b) You will have to buy a new battery

   c) It will erase all photographs stored on the laptop

   d) The laptop will shut down until you connect it to the main supply

Answers

Q1 – a, b and d   **Q2** – c   **Q3** – a, but it will be very useful for c

Q4 – c   **Q5** – d

PART I
Learning the Basics

Are you sure that's adequate anti-virus protection?

Getting started

1

Equipment needed: A computer running the Windows 8 operating system, monitor screen, preferably touchscreen, keyboard and mouse or trackpad.

Skills needed: Enthusiasm and an open mind.

Let's get started. This chapter is all about the basic mechanics of computer use. You will not be learning anything about day-to-day computing activities just yet but we all need to start somewhere when we learn a new skill, in the same way as the concert pianist has to learn the difference between the black and white keys and the learner driver has to learn the effects of the gear lever and clutch.

Having made the decision to plunge into the deep waters of computing, you now have your brand new machine sitting in front of you and are probably wondering what on earth you have let yourself in for. Don't worry. This book will put you in charge.

About Windows 8

Windows 8 is a radically new concept in the field of computing. Those of you who have used previous incarnations of the Windows operating system will have to adjust the way you think in order to adapt to the new system. On the other hand, beginners will have no previous concept of the use of Windows and may find the whole learning process easier. Windows 8 relies heavily on touchscreen technology, although it still allows you to use the familiar mouse and keyboard controls.

Turning the computer on

First of all, we are assuming that the following things have been done already: your guardian angel has set up your machine for you; all the necessary cables have been attached to the correct sockets; you have an Internet connection (even if you don't know what that is at the moment); and your computer is connected to the power supply.

Now we have to turn the thing on. Every machine has a power button — it's usually on the front of a desktop computer or above the keyboard of a laptop. It is typically identified by the power symbol (see Figure 1.1).

Figure 1.1

You will find a similar symbol on other equipment, such as additional screens, printers or scanners, so if you have any of these devices, switch them on at the same time. Such devices, as well as separate keyboards, mice and external storage discs, are known as *peripherals*. There is no separate power button for the integrated screen of a laptop. Press the button once and wait. A few lights will begin to flicker as the machine gets going. The screen may flash on and off a few times and you may see the computer manufacturer's logo. Within a few minutes or less, you will see the initial screen, known as the Lock screen (see Figure 1.2). This shows a pretty picture showing the date and time as well as a few small symbols along the bottom of the screen that show your computer's status — you don't need to know about these at this stage.

Figure 1.2

Your Lock screen may be different from the one illustrated — and the date and time will probably be wrong until your guardian angel has entered the correct settings.

Unlock the screen either by dragging the mouse pointer in an upwards direction or, if you have a touchscreen, by placing a finger on the screen and swiping upwards. The use of the mouse and finger gestures will be explained in a moment. If the computer has been set up with a password, the next screen will ask you to type it into the box. Press the Enter key and you're in!

The Start screen and Desktop screen

Windows 8 has two interfaces — the Start screen and the Desktop screen.

The Start screen or interface

The Start interface (see Figure 1.3) is the opening screen that is displayed when you have removed the Lock screen, so you should see this once you've input your password. This screen gives you access to everything you can do on the computer. The tiles on the Start screen are shortcuts to the various programs (called apps or applications) installed on the computer. To activate a tile, simply tap or click on it with the mouse button. We will be showing you how to use the Start interface in Chapter 2.

Figure 1.3

The Desktop screen or interface

The Desktop interface (see Figure 1.4) shows the shortcut icons, taskbar and a number of other control icons, all of which can be activated by tapping or clicking on the relevant icon. Those of you familiar with previous operating systems will recognise the layout. You will rarely see apps on the Desktop screen; one of its functions is to display shortcuts to larger programs (such as the full version of Internet Explorer to browse the web, Microsoft Excel to create spreadsheets, video editing software and home accounting systems). We explain how to use the Desktop interface in Chapter 3.

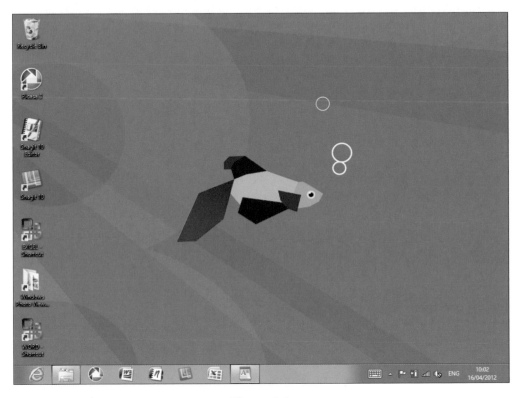

Figure 1.4

Apps and applications

What are *apps*? Are they the same as applications? And how do they differ from programs?

Apps are small (but often very powerful) computer programs on the Start screen that perform a specific task, such as finding a hotel, ordering from a store, accessing a particular newspaper or playing a game. Examples of apps would include Calendar, People (which gives you access to your address book) and Maps.

Programs are accessed from both the Start and Desktop interfaces, and tend to be much larger than apps. Confusingly, programs are also known as applications — not to be confused with apps! Programs (or applications) tend to offer a much broader range of options and include, for example, Microsoft Word (for creating letters and other documents), Microsoft Outlook (for emailing, calendars and contact lists) and Internet Explorer (for browsing the Internet). Where a photo manipulation *app* will remove red-eye from images or crop an image to a more suitable size, a photo manipulation *application* can refine and develop images in thousands of different ways. Similarly, you can use an *app* to post a short message on your Facebook page but will need a comprehensive word processing *application* to compose a detailed report, design a poster or write a novel.

Microsoft now uses the word 'application' to mean a 'program'. Both apps and applications appear as tiles on the Start screen, but the Desktop only shows the larger applications. In this book, we use the term 'apps' for the smaller programs and use the term 'applications' for the larger programs. In practice, you do not have to appreciate the finer differences between the two terms.

Controlling the computer

We have mentioned 'tapping', 'clicking', 'swiping' and 'dragging' and before we go any further you need to learn a little about controlling the computer. Windows 8 uses a number of methods of issuing commands to the computer. Commands can be given by using the touchscreen, mouse, trackpad and keyboard.

Touchscreen commands

Although Windows 8 can be operated by using the mouse and physical keyboard, it has been designed to use the emerging touchscreen technology already in use on mobile phones, tablets (such as the iPad) and netbooks. The touchscreen is operated using the following gestures. (Don't worry about what they do at this stage — it's enough just to be aware of what the gestures are.)

Swiping

To move the pointer using a touchscreen, drag a finger across the screen.

Tapping

To issue a command on a touchscreen, simply tap at an appropriate point on the screen. This may be a tile, a text box, an icon or a link to a web page.

Tap and hold

You may wish to move a tile to a different position on the Start screen. In this case, tap the tile but hold your finger against the screen while dragging the tile to its new position.

Flicking

You can scroll the screen both vertically and horizontally by flicking a finger up, down or across the screen. The faster the flick, the greater the movement across the screen:

● Flicking from the edges of the screen has different effects. To achieve this, place your finger on the edge of the screen frame and drag it quickly onto the screen.

● Flicking from the right edge reveals the Charms menu. (We'll explain this in Chapter 2.)

● Flicking from the left edge recovers the previous application. Using this gesture, you can scroll through all the open applications.

● Flicking from the top and bottom edges displays other relevant menus.

Pinching and stretching

Screen images can be enlarged or diminished by using these gestures. To enlarge a screen image, place a thumb and one finger on the screen or trackpad and 'stretch' them apart. To reduce the image, start with the thumb and finger apart and draw them together.

Although the iPad has a touchscreen, it uses a different operating system and does not work with Windows 8, although many of the commands may appear to be the same. For further information on the iPad, we recommend *iPad for the Older and Wiser* by Sean McManus, published by John Wiley & Sons, Inc.

The mouse

This small device comes in several different guises. Some are wired to the computer, as shown in Figure 1.5, while others are wireless; all have at least two buttons, left and right, and modern ones have a scroll wheel between the two. The purpose of the mouse is to move a pointer across the computer screen and issue commands at various points on the screen. You may have noticed the small white arrow pointer on the screen. This pointer is moved across the screen simply by moving the mouse across the surface of your desk. The action works best if the mouse is placed on a rubberised mouse pad. How well your mouse works will depend on the surface you place it on and the type of mouse. Some mice have a trackball that rotates as you move it whereas others have a red laser that controls the movement. It needs to be on a clean, level surface.

Figure 1.5

Clicking

When using a mouse, commands are given by placing the pointer at a certain point on the screen and pressing — or 'clicking' — the left mouse button while holding the mouse perfectly still with the palm of the hand. For example, you may have created an email that you wish to send. Somewhere on the screen will be the word 'Send'. By moving the pointer to the word and clicking the left mouse button, you will give the command to send the document. This action is known as a 'left-click'.

The right button has a completely different effect in that it raises a menu that is context-sensitive. We discuss the use of the right-click in later chapters.

Try using the mouse to move the pointer around the screen. Like riding a bicycle for the first time, this will take a little practice but familiarity will come eventually. You can adjust the size of the pointer and the way it moves, and we will cover this in Chapter 5.

In certain situations, you may need to perform a double-click, using the left mouse button. This can prove difficult for beginners. This is because they tend to hold the mouse very rigidly with the result that the mouse moves imperceptibly between the two clicks leading the computer to interpret the command as two single clicks. Try steadying the mouse with the palm of your hand while operating the button with the forefinger. Double-clicking is much easier when using a laptop trackpad instead of a mouse. We discuss the trackpad in a moment. (Once again, the function of the double-click is adjustable.)

Practice exercises using the mouse and touchscreen gestures are explained in Chapter 7.

When this book instructs you to 'click', this always means the left mouse button. Similarly, 'double-clicking' always means the left button. The right mouse button always brings up a menu. There is *never* a double right-click. Dragging is almost always done using the left button.

Dragging

The second mouse action is known as 'dragging', which you can try now. If you still have the Start screen showing (as in Figure 1.3), place the mouse pointer at the bottom of the screen, hold down the left mouse button and move the pointer from right to left across the screen. This will have the effect of dragging further tiles across the screen, and will reveal more square and rectangular tiles. We'll discuss the functions of these in Chapter 2.

The scroll wheel lying between the two buttons allows you to scroll a long document up and down the screen.

Just as a practice exercise, place the pointer over the Calendar tile and left-click. This will open up the Calendar app in the form of a diary. To return to the Start screen, simply press the Windows key — this is the key that looks like a segmented flag, at the bottom left of the standard keyboard. More about the keyboard in a few moments.

The trackpad

Laptop computers are more usually controlled by means of a trackpad, which is a touch-sensitive square that sits below the typing keys on the keyboard. The track-pad controls the pointer in much the same way as the mouse (see Figure 1.6). The screen pointer is moved by dragging a finger up, down, side to side and across and even diagonally across the trackpad. If you reach the side of the pad before you have finished moving the pointer, simply lift your finger and start again from the other side.

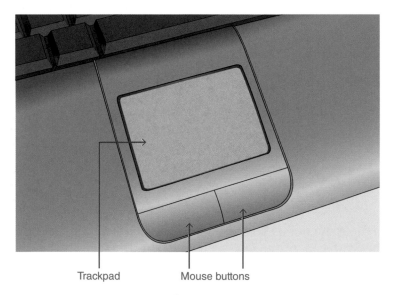

Trackpad   Mouse buttons

Figure 1.6

The control buttons lie below the pad and fulfil the same functions as the mouse buttons. Drag the pointer by holding down the left button with one finger while moving the pointer with a finger of the other hand on the trackpad. Only use a single finger when using the trackpad to move the pointer around the screen — using two fingers or more can confuse the machine. Many trackpads will also accept 'stretching' gestures to alter the size of a window.

The standard keyboard

So far, we have concentrated on commands that move or activate the screen tiles. However, much of your computer use will involve typing text and this is where the keyboard comes in. The keyboard simply gives commands to the computer. These commands may be as simple as typing the letter 'a' or inserting a paragraph in a letter, or as complicated as creating a photograph that looks like an oil painting.

Windows 8 allows you to use two different types of keyboard: standard and virtual. We'll come back to the virtual keyboard later, but for now let us look at the standard keyboard that is attached to your computer.

Figure 1.7 shows a standard keyboard from a personal computer. Laptop keyboards are more compact and often don't include a number pad, page command block (to the left of the number pad) or direction keys.

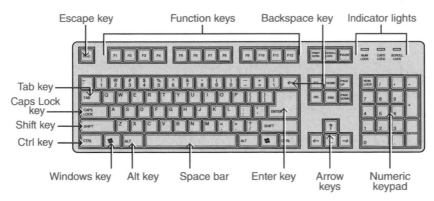

Figure 1.7

The layout of your keyboard will depend on the type and model of computer you are using but they all have a similar basic layout, based on old manual typewriters, known as the QWERTY layout (after the first six letter keys on the top row). The letters and numbers in this central section of the keyboard act in the same way as a typewriter.

27

The letter keys are surrounded by an array of additional keys, often with confusing labels such as Alt, Ctrl, PrtScr or F4. By exploring these keys in manageable chunks, their functions will become more understandable.

The Enter key

The Enter key (sometimes called the Return key) is found to the right of the letter keys (see Figure 1.7). When you're typing a document, this key creates a new line below the previous text in the same way as a carriage return does on a typewriter. By pressing this key twice you will create a blank line. But there is more to the Enter key than this — it is one of the most important keys on the keyboard. It issues commands to the computer in many different ways, as we shall see as we progress through this book. As an example, you will often be presented with a number of options with one of the alternatives highlighted (this is known as the default action, which we will discuss later in the book). In Figure 1.8, the 'Yes' option is high-lighted; this is the 'default' command that is activated if you press the Enter key.

Figure 1.8

The Windows key

You will find this key towards the left end of the lowest line of keys on the keyboard (see Figure 1.7). The Windows key has a very different function in Windows 8 to the one it had in previous Windows systems: now, hitting this key always returns you to the Start screen. Hitting the Windows key when the Start screen is already displayed will take you to whichever screen you had open previously. This feature is known as a toggle switch. We shall be making more use of this key in Chapter 2.

The Tab key

As on a typewriter, this key (see Figure 1.7) tabulates columns by moving the text entry point a set distance to the right, as shown here.

Jan
Feb
Mar
Apr
May
Jun
Jul   Aug

103
24
456
67
9
239
1056   18

The computer also finds other uses for this key, as we shall discover in later chapters.

The Backspace key

This key is a relic of the old typewriter. On a computer, while it still takes the typing point back one space, it also deletes the character to the *left* of the typing point. This key can vary in position on the keyboard but is usually found in the upper-right quadrant of the keyboard (see Figure 1.7).

The Delete key

This key can be confused with the Backspace key. As its name suggests, it removes things from the screen, including text, but in this case, it removes characters to the *right* of the typing point. Once again, its position on the keyboard is not set in stone but it is usually found towards the right of the keyboard (see Figure 1.7).

The Escape key

The Esc key (short for Escape) is always found at the top-left corner of the keyboard (see Figure 1.7). It has many different functions depending on the situation but can be seen as the 'get out of jail free' key — sometimes! It does not always work as you would expect. If you have initiated a computer process that seems to be running out of control, pressing this key will often bring the process to a shuddering halt with sighs of relief all round. It will not stop the computer, only the runaway process. However, it is not a good idea to rely too heavily on this key.

Modifying keys

Some keys (the Shift keys, Caps Lock key, Ctrl key and Alt key) are known as modifying keys. These are keys that do nothing on their own but are always used in conjunction with other keys to modify their action. These keys are

● **Shift keys:** There are two of these keys, one at each end of the letter keys (see Figure 1.7). They each perform the same function in that, when held down while pressing another key, they print the uppercase character (in the same way as the Caps key on a typewriter). Thus, pressing down the Shift key and hitting the 'p' key (normally written as Shift+p) will result in a capital P; and Shift+7 will produce the ampersand (&) character. Like many other computing keys, the Shift key is used in many different ways by more advanced computer programs but that need not worry us at the moment.

Most new computers no longer have the word Shift on the Shift key, but an upwards arrow.

● **Caps Lock key:** Why keyboard manufacturers persist in using the term Caps Lock when they have changed the Caps key to Shift is quite beyond us! The Caps Lock key sits with the Shift key on the left of the keyboard (see Figure 1.7), which sometimes leads to confusion among novice students. Unlike the Shift key, the Caps Lock is a 'toggle' key: if you press this key, all the letters you type will appear in capital letters. Press it again, and they will be in lowercase letters. It's easier to use the Shift key if you only want to capitalise individual characters, and you always have to use the Shift key to use the uppercase symbols on the number keys.

● **Ctrl key:** No, it's not a typing error — Ctrl is keyboard-speak for Control. This modifying key is used by many programs to issue commands. For instance, in many word processing applications, holding down the Ctrl key while hitting the

P key (Ctrl+P) will issue the command to print the document. Ctrl+Z usually reverses the action of the last command given. There are two Ctrl keys on the keyboard, one at each end, both performing the same functions (see Figure 1.7).

● **Alt key:** This key allows you to change (or alternate) the function of other keys in a similar way to the Ctrl key, and is used to issue keyboard commands. For instance, Alt Gr +C produces the copyright symbol © when using the Microsoft Word program.

The modifying keys can be used in combination with each other to give well over 300 command shortcuts, of which only about a dozen are of practical use to the average computer user. There is a table of the most useful keyboard shortcuts in Chapter 9 but don't worry about remembering these combinations for now — it is just the principle we are trying to establish at this stage. You are probably having enough difficulty just locating the apostrophe key. (It is probably under the @ symbol to the right of the letter keys if you are still searching.)

Those of you with limited keyboards on smaller computers may notice that some keys carry a third symbol. A common one is the euro (€) symbol. These additional characters are produced by holding down the Alt key, the Ctrl key and the symbol key at the same time.

The Function keys

These are the keys labelled F1 to F12 that run across the top of the keyboard, as you can see Figure 1.7 (most laptop keyboards add additional symbols to these keys to extend their capabilities). Depending on the keyboard layout, you may have to use a further modifying key, the Fn key, to activate these keys. There is no need to go into the various uses of these keys at this stage except to mention that most computer programs use the F1 key to raise a help menu if you find yourself stuck with a problem. There will be more on the various Help facilities in Chapter 9.

Try to break it!

As we mentioned in the Introduction, beginners are often afraid that they might break the computer. Short of using a sledgehammer or pouring a cup of coffee onto the machine, computers are remarkable robust. If you need reassurance about that, try this exercise. Press the palm of one hand on the keyboard several times. Did anything happen? Do it again, and again. Now use both hands. It's possible that something may appear on the screen — in the case of Windows 8, most likely a meaningless jumble of letters or a menu (in which case, simply press the Esc key and/or the Start key and everything will revert to normal). Whatever happens, you will not have caused damage to the computer.

The virtual keyboards

Windows 8 offers an alternative method of entering text, by using keyboards that appear on the screen. There is not enough room to accommodate all the keys on one screen, so you may have to switch between different layouts to find the key you require.

Figure 1.9 shows the initial virtual keyboard, which is largely used for typing the letters of the alphabet. Type by tapping or clicking on the keys to produce the required lowercase characters. To produce a capital letter, tap or click either of the Shift keys followed by the letter key. Double tapping or clicking on the Shift keys locks the keys into uppercase mode. To exit the uppercase mode, simply tap or click one of the Shift keys again.

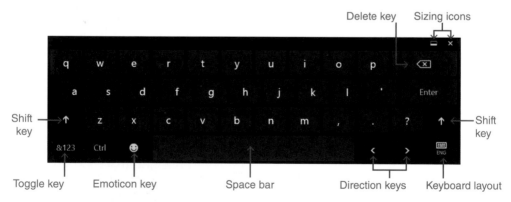

Figure 1.9

The Delete key functions as a Backspace key and as a Delete key while the emoticon key offers a selection of smiley faces and other symbols.

The keyboard layout key allows you to alter the appearance of the keyboard.

Access to different keyboards offering numerals and other characters is provided by the keypad toggle key labelled &123 (see Figures 1.10 and 1.11).

Additional keyboards

Figure 1.10

Figure 1.11

Turning the computer off

Unfortunately, Microsoft has made the process of turning the computer off using Windows 8 rather more complicated than using previous operating systems. Different computers will shut down in different ways, but don't panic — there is one sure-fire method of doing it properly. You will need to use some of the skills described in this chapter to shut your computer down. Here is a step-by-step guide:

1. Either swipe your finger from the far right edge of the touch-screen or place the mouse pointer at the top-right corner of the screen. Either action will bring up the Charms menu (see Figure 1.12).

2. The Charms menu displays five alternative icons, all of which will be described in Chapter 2. For the purposes of this exercise we are only interested in the Settings option.

3. Either touch the word Settings or move the mouse pointer over it and left-click on it.

4. This brings up an additional menu (see Figure 1.13), which includes an option labelled Power. Tap this option or left-click on it and a further list of menu options will appear, including the option to Shut Down. Tap this option or touch it with your finger and the computer will shut down automatically within a few minutes or less.

Figure 1.12

Figure 1.13

There are easier methods to close the computer down but these involve setting your computer up to allow these actions. This will be covered in Chapter 6, which deals with setting up your computer to reflect your personal preferences.

That is quite enough for you to assimilate for now so I suggest you go and make yourself a strong cup of coffee before moving on to the specialised subject of the computer screen. Don't try to learn everything at one sitting — this book and the computer will still be there in the morning.

Summary

- Windows 8 is a very different operating system to the ones that preceded it.

- Turning the computer on is very simple. It is more complicated to turn it off.

- You can give commands to the computer using a touchscreen, mouse or keyboard.

- Move the mouse with the palm of your hand and do not grip it too tightly.

- Laptops tend to use a trackpad rather than a mouse.

- The keyboard is simply an extension of the old typewriter layout with specialist computer keys added.

- The Enter key activates computer commands as well as adding additional lines to a text document.

- The modifying keys only act in association with other keys.

- Computers are very difficult to break.

- Don't worry about making mistakes. They are valuable teaching tools.

Brain training

There may be more than one correct answer to a question.

1. Which key should be used to start the computer?

a) The Enter key

b) The Windows key

c) The power button

d) No key is needed, you simply have to attach the power cable

2. What happens if you press the Shift key on its own?

a) Nothing

b) It converts all the keys to uppercase

c) You move the power supply from mains to battery

d) The keyboard prints symbols instead of letters

3. What is the action of the Windows key?

a) It brings up the Charms menu

b) It toggles the screen between the Start interface and previous open window

c) The computer will close down

d) It connects you to the Windows website

4. What is a trackpad?

a) A pointing device on a desktop computer

b) An alternative to a mouse on a laptop computer

c) A device for recording your key strokes

d) A touch-sensitive area on a keyboard

5. What happens when you use the Backspace key?

a) You remove the previous line of type

b) It removes characters to the left of the typing point

c) It deletes characters to the right of the typing point

d) It creates more space at the top of a document

Answers

Q1 – c   **Q2** – a   **Q3** – b

Q4 – b and d   **Q5** – b

2

Using the Start screen

Equipment needed: A computer, Windows 8 operating system, screen, preferably with touchscreen facility, mouse or keypad.

Skills needed: Some knowledge of the use of the mouse, trackpad and touchscreen (Chapter 1); patience and enthusiasm to learn.

The Start screen is the new way that Microsoft displays applications on your computer. If you have used previous versions of Windows, the interface will appear strange, but it is quite easy to use.

The Lock screen

In Chapter 1, we mentioned the Lock screen, which is the first screen to appear when you start up the computer. Your computer will also display this screen if it has been standing idle for a time and lapsed into sleep mode to conserve power. To wake up the 'sleeping' computer, swipe a finger up the screen or drag the mouse pointer from bottom to top (see Figure 2.1).

Swipe direction

Figure 2.1

If your computer has been set up with a user password you will need to enter this into the text box on the next screen, then press or tap the Enter key.

Having a password is a wise precaution to prevent unauthorised access to your computer and its contents. Passwords should consist of at least eight characters, which can be a mixture of upper and lowercase letters, numbers and symbols. We will be discussing the subject of security in Chapter 11.

The Start menu

After pressing the Enter key, you will be presented with the Start screen (see Figure 2.2). You can also access the Start screen using the mouse or trackpad by placing the pointer at the bottom-left corner of the screen and clicking the left mouse button. We had a glimpse of this screen in Chapter 1. Now is the time to investigate it further.

Figure 2.2

Tiles

Tiles are the access points to the various apps and applications installed on your computer. When you first view your Start screen it will not look exactly like Figure 2.2. The tiles will be in a different order, they may vary in size and there will be fewer of them but the principles we are going to describe remain the same. As you can see in the image, there are more tiles off to the right of the screen. To view these, simply drag a finger — or the mouse pointer — across the screen from right to left. You can reverse the process to view the original tiles by dragging in the opposite direction.

Display all the Start menu tiles on a single screen by right-clicking on the Start screen or by flicking a finger down from the top edge of the screen and then clicking the All Apps button.

Arranging the tiles

You will probably want to see the files that you use the most at the left end of the tile block, so that they are the ones that are easiest for you to access. This is very easily achieved by dragging a tile to the required position. As you drag the tile in question the other tiles will move to make way for the dragged tile. Once the tile is in the desired position, remove your finger from the screen. Continue with this process until you have arranged the tiles to your satisfaction.

Sizing the tiles

There are two available tile sizes — smaller squares and larger rectangles. You may wish to show those tiles that you use on a regular basis as large rectangles for easier viewing. Right-click on the tile to access a menu to do this. This is done in one of two ways, by using either the mouse or the touchscreen:

● If you have a mouse or trackpad, just place the pointer over the tile and right-click.

● To effect a right-click using the touchscreen, tap and hold your finger on the tile until the menu appears at the bottom of the screen.

The resulting menu (shown in Figure 2.3) allows you to unpin or remove the tile from the Start screen, uninstall the app, alter the size of the tile or turn the live tile off. The following list describes these actions:

Figure 2.3

● **Unpinning and uninstalling:** Tapping the Unpin from Start icon only removes the tile from the Start screen. Uninstalling removes the app from the computer altogether, so take care when using this.

- **Resizing the tiles:** Clicking or tapping on the sizing button will change the size of the tile.

- **Turning the live tile off:** Some of the tiles on the Start screen can display live information. For instance, if you have set the Weather app to show details of your local forecast, the tile will show the current weather at your chosen locality. A live Calendar tile will show your next appointment and the Mail tile will show your latest email message. These live tiles can be an irritant and can also make identification of the tiles more difficult. You can disable this feature using the Turn Live Tile Off icon.

To remove the menu, right-click or press and hold the activated tile.

Opening and closing apps

The tiles are effectively shortcuts to the apps. Simply tap or left-click on a tile to activate the app.

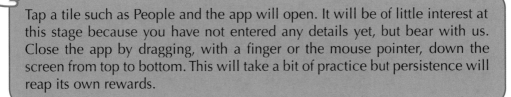

Tap a tile such as People and the app will open. It will be of little interest at this stage because you have not entered any details yet, but bear with us. Close the app by dragging, with a finger or the mouse pointer, down the screen from top to bottom. This will take a bit of practice but persistence will reap its own rewards.

Windows 8 does not restrict you to having one app open at a time. When you closed the first app, you will have been returned to the Start screen. (If this is not visible, hit the Windows key.) We are now going to open a number of apps. Once again, tap the People app but, this time, do not close it. Press the Windows key to return to the Start menu and tap another tile such as Maps. Ignore the app for the moment and hit the Windows key again then tap or click on a third tile.

You have now opened three apps. But where are they?

You can reveal the list of open apps in one of two ways. Place the mouse pointer at the top-left corner of the screen and you will see a small window or thumbnail image of the last app you opened. Keep the pointer against the left edge of the screen and move it down. Doing this opens up the thumbnails of the open apps (see Figure 2.4). Clicking or tapping on one of these thumbnails will expand the app to the full screen. With the list of thumbnails in view, you can close an open app by right-clicking on the thumbnail and left-clicking on the Close option.

Figure 2.4

To open the apps list using the touchscreen requires a different gesture. Swipe a finger from the left edge of the screen, maintain contact with the screen and move the finger back towards the edge. Once again, this action will reveal the column of open apps.

You do not have to display the open app list to reveal an open app. You can 'cycle' through them by repeatedly flicking from the left edge of the screen.

Touchscreen gestures can feel awkward at first but follow Robert the Bruce's famous adage and try, try and try again.

All open apps will close when the computer is shut down.

Charms

The Charms menu, shown in Figure 2.5, which has five options, is revealed by swiping from the right edge of the screen. If you are restricted to a mouse, open it by placing the pointer in the top-right corner of the screen. We have already seen this menu in Chapter 1, when we used it to shut down the computer. It is now time to investigate this menu in greater depth.

Figure 2.5

Search

This charm allows you to search the computer for apps, settings and files. The initial screen shows all the apps installed on the computer. If you see the app you are looking for, simply click or tap on it as you would have done on the Start menu. Otherwise, type a search term into the text box to display the apps that match your search.

Share

The Share charm allows you to send content from your computer to other people or other computers in a simple way. Let's say you are browsing through your photos on the computer and you discover one you would like to share with your friends. Windows 8 has made this process quite simple. With the photo app running, select the photo or photos that you wish to share, then click the Share icon on the Charms menu. You will now see a screen that tells you which apps can share this photo. Select Mail, type in the name of the recipient and then type any message you wish to include (see Figure 2.6).

Figure 2.6

Click the Send icon and that's it. Not all apps can share but Windows 8 will tell you what is and isn't available when you use the Share button. (Emailing will be covered in Chapter 12.)

Start

This charm may seem a little redundant as it performs the same action as pressing the Windows key — it opens up the Start menu.

Devices

This charm allows the computer to communicate with other devices such as printers, other computers, television sets and audio systems. At this stage in your computing career, we suggest that you leave these options to your guardian angel.

Settings

The Settings charm is probably the most useful charm at this stage (see Figure 2.7). A quick way of getting to this screen is to use the Windows key + the letter I. Let us investigate some of its functions.

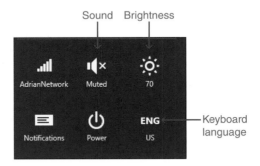

Figure 2.7

Network

This gives you information about the computer's connection to the outside world and the Internet. The two headings here mention Flight mode and Wi-Fi .If the Flight mode is turned on, don't worry — your wireless connection will not interfere with an aircraft's controls! You only need to use this option if you intend to use your laptop or tablet while travelling at 35,000 feet. The Wi-Fi heading will show you which wireless networks are visible from the computer.

Sound

Using this icon, you can alter the volume of the computer's speakers. Tap or click on the icon to show a volume bar. By dragging the setting point to the very bottom you will mute the speaker completely.

Brightness

This icon (the one that looks like a sun) allows you to increase or decrease the brightness of the screen. A very bright screen is likely to drain the battery of a laptop or tablet at a faster rate than normal. Alter the setting by dragging the setting point up and down the 'thermometer' bar. A setting of between 50 and 70 will allow a reasonable compromise between readability and battery life.

Notifications

Notifications from various apps can appear as pop-up windows at the top-right corner of the screen. This setting allows you to prevent these from appearing for a period of time.

Power

This charm allows you to shut down or restart the computer or send it into sleep mode to save battery power.

Keyboard language

Windows 8 can accommodate a large number of different keyboard languages. Note that one of the main differences between the English (US) or English (UK) options is that the @ symbol and the quote marks symbol (found above the 2 key) are reversed. Some computers may come with only one language loaded. It is a simple job for your guardian angel to download other languages from the Internet to make them available on your computer. Click or tap on this key to select your language of choice.

Change PC Settings

Tapping on this text at the foot of the Charms menu opens up a huge range of options that allow you to customise the computer to your own personal choices. We shall be covering this subject later in Chapter 6. At this stage it is sufficient only for you to know that you will be using this facility to change the Lock screen picture and background colour, create user images, create additional users of the computer, change your password, set the date and time and much more.

Searching the computer

Windows 8 has adopted a radically new method of searching the contents of the computer. We have already seen the Search option in the Charms menu but there is a faster way of finding that elusive app, photo or file hidden away in the depths of the computer.

With the Start menu in view (press the Windows key if it is not visible), start typing.

Figure 2.8 shows the results when we typed the word "power" into the Start screen. Underneath the search term on the right of the screen, you can see that it has found two apps, 10 settings and 12 files, all of which contain the search term. On the left is a list revealing that the two apps are PowerShell and Microsoft Office PowerPoint. By clicking or tapping on the Settings icon in the list on the right, the 10 options settings will be displayed; this will allow you to alter the power settings, change when the computer goes into sleep mode or change the battery settings. Similarly, you can select the Files icon to reveal the 12 files that include the word "power".

Figure 2.8

Start typing a word of your choice to see what information you can gather. You do not have to type a complete word. By typing in 'ven' you won't find any apps or settings but you may discover photos with 'Venice' in the file name or a letter file containing the word 'event'. As you continue typing the word, you will see the number of results changing so you may not need to complete the word before you find what you are looking for. The longer the word, the more accurate the search result.

Summary

- The Lock screen prevents unauthorised access to the computer.

- The Start screen displays tiles that access apps.

- You can return to the Start screen at any time by pressing the Windows key or placing the mouse pointer at the bottom-left corner of the screen and clicking.

- Open an app by tapping or clicking on the relevant tile.

- Close an app by dragging a finger down the screen.

- You can have several different apps open at the same time.

- To view open apps, drag a finger from the left edge of the screen, maintain contact and swipe back to the left. Using the mouse pointer, point to the upper-left corner and move it down the left edge of the screen.

- The Charms menu allows you to customise the display, alter the sound settings and shut the computer down.

- Search for apps, settings and files by using the Search facility in the Charms menu or simply typing a search term onto the Start screen.

Brain training

There may be more than one correct answer to the questions.

1. How do you alter the arrangement of the Start menu tiles?

   a)   Use the Charms menu

   b)   Right-click on the tile

   c)   Use a finger to drag the tile to a new position

   d)   Place the mouse pointer on the tile, hold down the left mouse button and drag the tile to a new position

2. How would you close an app?

   a)   Right-click and choose Close

   b)   Drag a finger sharply down the screen from top to bottom

   c)   Drag the screen to the left

   d)   Use the Esc key

3. How can you display a list of open apps?

   a)   Place the mouse pointer at the top-left corner and move it down the edge of the screen

   b)   Drag a finger from the left edge of the screen and back again

   c)   Flick down from the top edge of the screen

   d)   Press the Enter key

4. How would you discover how to change what happens when you close the lid of a laptop?

   a)   You do not have this option

   b)   This can only be achieved by a qualified computer engineer

   c)   Type the word "lid" onto the Start screen

   d)   Use the Search facility in the Charms menu

Answers

Q1 – c and d   **Q2** – b

Q3 – a and b   **Q4** – c and d

Using the Desktop interface

3

Equipment needed: A computer with monitor screen, preferably with touchscreen facility, Windows 8 operating system, keyboard and mouse or trackpad.

Skills needed: Some knowledge of the keyboard, mouse or trackpad (Chapter 1) and a willingness to make mistakes.

Windows 8 offers two different screens, or interfaces. We discussed the Start screen in Chapter 2. If you are accustomed to touchscreen devices, such as the iPad or touchscreen phones, you will have noticed that the Start screen has some similarities with these. But the interface may have been a completely new experience for some of you who are familiar with previous Windows incarnations, such as Windows XP and Windows 7. If this is true for you, take heart — the familiar Desktop screen is still available on Windows 8, albeit with a few modifications.

The Start screen, while operable by a mouse or trackpad, is primarily designed for touchscreen use. The Desktop screen will also accept many of the touchscreen gestures but is more adapted to use with the traditional mouse or touchpad. Many applications (or programs) will automatically switch into Desktop mode when opened from the Start screen.

One of the tiles on the Start menu is labelled Desktop (see Figure 3.1).

Figure 3.1

Tap or click on this tile to reveal the familiar Windows Desktop (see Figure 3.2).

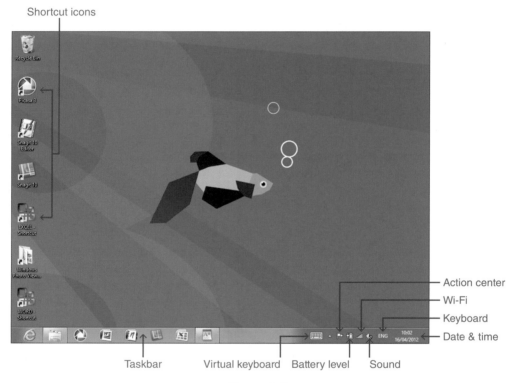

Figure 3.2

The major omission from the Desktop screen in Windows 8 is the Start button at the left end of the taskbar. This will not be a problem to those who have just begun their computing experience with Windows 8.

Microsoft is now referring to programs as 'applications'. Applications are not the same thing as apps. Apps tend to be smaller and subject-specific, and are found on the Start screen (discussed in Chapter 2).

Icons

Icons are essentially shortcuts to various programs, or 'applications'. To open an application from the Desktop screen, double-tap or double-click on the shortcut icon.

These icons normally run down the left side of the Desktop screen but they can be moved to suit your own preferences. To place an icon in a different position on the screen, place the pointer on the icon, hold down the left mouse button and drag it to the position of choice.

Your new Desktop will not show as many icons as are shown in Figure 3.2. More icons will gradually be added to the Desktop as you install further applications.

Recycle bin

This is one icon you will certainly see on your Desktop. It offers an invaluable safety net to prevent you from accidentally losing files or programs. If you delete a file or uninstall a program or application, it is not immediately cast into outer-space but is stored in the Recycle bin. If you have deleted a file in error, you can retrieve it by opening the bin and restoring the file.

You can empty the Recycle bin by right-clicking on the Recycle bin icon and choosing to Empty Recycle bin.

Once you have emptied the Recycle bin you will no longer be able to restore deleted files. They may not have been completely lost but it would need a forensic computer engineer to recover the files. So before emptying the bin, make sure there's nothing in it you want to keep.

Taskbar

This runs along the bottom of the screen and contains faster shortcuts to your most commonly used applications (see Figure 3.2). They are faster because they are always visible in whatever application is running and only require a single tap or click to activate them.

Initially there will only be one or two icons on the taskbar, such as the Internet Explorer and Libraries icons (see Figure 3.3). To add a shortcut to the taskbar, simply drag a shortcut icon from the main screen onto the taskbar and release the left mouse button or lift your finger.

Figure 3.3

System Tray

The group of icons at the right end of the taskbar is collectively described as the System Tray (see Figure 3.2).

Virtual keyboard

Selecting this icon displays a screen keyboard for use with touchscreen computers such as laptops and tablets. The virtual keyboard may not be visible but can be added to the taskbar by using the right mouse button and selecting Toolbars.

Action centre

This is where notification of any available updates or security issues will appear.

Battery level and Wi-Fi status

The current state of your battery level and Internet connection are shown on both the Lock screen and the Charms menu, but they are also shown on the Desktop screen. Hovering the pointer over the battery icon will reveal the level of charge remaining.

Sound

Control of your computer's sound system is even easier on the Desktop than on the Start screen. Simply tap or click on the small loudspeaker icon to alter the volume level or mute the speakers completely.

Keyboard

This allows you to alter the language of the keyboard in the same way as the keyboard language icon in the Charms menu.

Date and time

Tapping or clicking on this icon raises a small window that allows you to set the correct time and date (see Figure 3.4). This is significantly easier and faster to do on the Desktop than on the Start screen.

Figure 3.4

Organising the Desktop

After a while you will begin to accumulate a number of shortcut icons. Some of these will be important, while others will be of little or no value. To personalise the desktop to your own requirements, you need to access a menu of options. Place the mouse pointer on a blank area of the Desktop and right-click.

The initial menu offers a number of options. In Figure 3.5, the View option has been selected, which allows you to arrange the icons, alter their size and add any gadgets that may be available. Gadgets are small windows displayed on the Desktop, which display real-time information about the weather, incoming mail, to-do lists and much more. (No gadgets are shown in the figures in this chapter.)

The Sort By option allows you to arrange the icons by size, type, date and name; the New option gives you the opportunity to add folders, files and other shortcuts to the desktop screen, and the Personalize option allows you to alter the colour scheme, background, mouse pointers and sounds of the computer (see Figure 3.6).

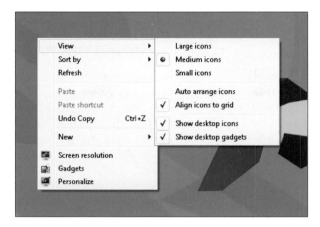

Figure 3.5

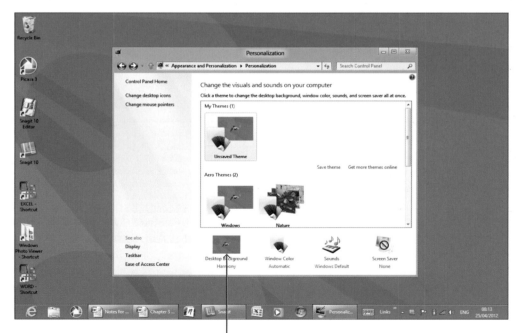

Background icon

Figure 3.6

To change the background image, place the mouse pointer on a blank area of the Desktop and right-click to activate the menu in Figure 3.5, and choose Personalize. Left-click or tap on the Desktop Background icon. This displays a further screen, as shown in Figure 3.7.

Click on the Browse button, navigate your way to the picture you want to use as your background and open it. Click on Apply and finally click on OK. (If you have trouble navigating to the picture, we will be explaining how to navigate the file system in Chapter 5.)

Figure 3.7

Organising the taskbar

Right-clicking on the taskbar raises a different menu relating only to the taskbar. Remember that a right-click always raises a context-sensitive menu — in other words, a menu that is sensitive to the area of the screen identified by the mouse pointer. This menu offers the options of adding further features to the taskbar. Play around with these options to find out what suits your personal requirements.

Jump lists

Initially, the icons 'pinned' to the taskbar will simply allow you to open the application and start work. Once you have created a file or two using one of these applications, the computer remembers the files you used most recently. To access one of these files, simply right-click on the Library icon (normally found towards the left of the taskbar) and a 'jump list' will appear, showing the files you accessed most recently (see Figure 3.8). Left-click on the file you want and it will open ready for further work. (We will talk more about files and folders in Chapter 5.)

Figure 3.8

Multitasking

You can have a number of apps and Desktop applications running at the same time. Reveal the open applications by placing the pointer at the top-left corner of the screen and move it down the left side to show the active applications. A link to the Start screen also appears at the bottom-left corner of this list of active applications.

Aero Peek

The Desktop interface also offers another way of multitasking called Aero Peek (see Figure 3.9). This is useful, for instance, if you are working on three documents at the same time. There is not enough room to show them along the taskbar but if you hover the pointer over the multitasking application in question, a list of the open files will appear, allowing you to left-click on a file without having to close the previous one.

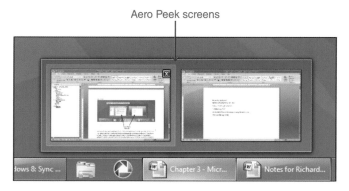

Figure 3.9

Show the Desktop

If you have a number of applications open on the Desktop, you can clear the screen to show the full Desktop by moving the pointer to the very bottom-right corner of the screen. (It must be in the corner rather than on the edge, as this would raise the Charms menu.) To return to the open application, simply move the pointer away from the corner. To maintain the full view of the Desktop, left-click in the corner: the open applications will remain open but will be minimised on the taskbar. This action can sometimes confuse the beginner who accidentally moves the mouse to that corner and thinks they have 'lost' the active application screen!

Summary

- The Start screen is better adapted to touch gestures; the Desktop screen will be more familiar to users of previous Windows systems who might be more comfortable using a mouse or trackpad.

- The screen icons are simply shortcuts to programs, or 'applications', in the same way that tiles are used on the Start screen. They are activated by tapping or clicking on them in the same way.

- The Recycle bin retains deleted folders and files for future retrieval until it has deliberately been emptied.

- Right-clicking on the Desktop allows organisation of the Desktop.

- The Desktop screen can be personalised to your own choice of colour scheme, background images and icon placement.

- Active applications are always accessible by moving the pointer to the top-left corner of the screen before moving it down the left side of the screen.

- The taskbar displays frequently used application icons as well as system information.

- Jump lists offer access to recently activated files.

- Aero Peek shows the open files of any particular application.

Brain training

There may be more than one correct answer to the following questions.

1. **What is the difference between Start screen tiles and Desktop icons?**

   a) Tiles are operated by touch and icons by mouse clicks

   b) Not a lot — they both open applications

   c) Icons for Windows apps do not appear on the Desktop

   d) Desktop icons require a double-click while the tiles respond to a single tap or click

2. **How would you add the virtual keyboard to the taskbar?**

   a) Right-click the taskbar and then select toolbars

   b) Right-click on the desktop and select Personalize

   c) Double-click the taskbar

   d) You cannot add the virtual keyboard to the taskbar

3. **How would you change the appearance of the Desktop?**

   a) Right-click on the screen and choose Personalize

   b) Use the Settings tile on the Start screen

   c) Right-click on the taskbar and select Personalize

   d) You will need the supplier to organise this for you

4. **An active window suddenly disappears from the Desktop screen. What has happened?**

   a) You have closed the application

   b) The battery has run low

   c) You have moved the mouse pointer to the bottom-right corner of the screen

   d) You have moved the mouse pointer to the top-left corner of the screen

Answers

Q1 – b, c and d   **Q2** – a

Q3 – a and b   **Q4** – a and c

Using windows

4

Equipment needed: A computer (laptop or desktop), Windows 8 operating system and monitor screen, preferably with a touch-screen facility, keyboard and mouse or trackpad.

Skills needed: Experience with keyboard and mouse (Chapter 1) and the Desktop screen (Chapter 3).

In Windows 8, applications that run in Desktop mode are displayed as a window (unlike apps running from the Start screen, which use the full extent of the screen).

This chapter describes what a computing window looks like, and how to manipulate it and identify its various parts.

All previous Microsoft operating systems have displayed programs (or applications) as 'windows'. Windows 8 offers two methods of displaying applications. All Desktop applications operate within a window, so it is essential that you know how to use a window.

The structure of a window

The basic structure of all windows is similar so let us activate a window to discuss its anatomy. To display a simple window, click or tap on the Desktop tile on the Start screen and then tap or click on the Library icon towards the left end of the taskbar.

Study Figure 4.1 carefully to familiarise yourself with the various areas and their labels, which are common to all windows. We will explain the various features from top to bottom.

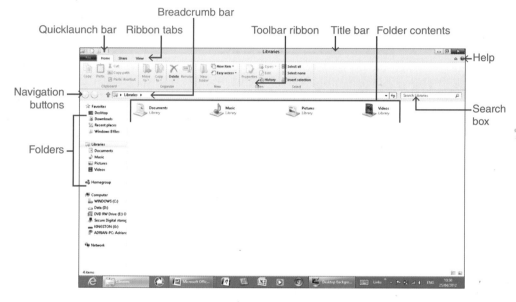

Figure 4.1

Title bar

This lies along the very top of the window and usually displays the name of the application that is currently operating. The window in Figure 4.1 is simply labelled 'Libraries' because it is not an application as such but a list of folders. We will see a window operating an application in Chapter 8, but at this stage, we are only concerned with the principle. If the window does not completely fill the screen, tap or click on the middle button of the sizing buttons at the top right of the window.

Quicklaunch bar

At the left of the title bar is the Quicklaunch bar, which gives you access to some of the commands that are more frequently used.

Sizing buttons

These three buttons lie at the right of the Title bar (see Figure 4.2). They allow you to change the size of the window or close the application completely. The left button (the one that looks like a minus sign) minimises the window to the taskbar at the bottom of the screen. Although minimising closes the window the application will still be running — all you are doing is getting it out of the way, keeping it running and available to use whenever you need it. The central button (which is a single square when the window is not maximised) maximises the window to fill the screen. When the window is maximised this button changes to become two superimposed squares (as in Figure 4.1). Click this to restore the window to its smaller size. Once a screen is maximised you will lose sight of all other windows that are currently open. The final button (the cross on the right) closes the application completely.

Figure 4.2

Be careful when using the Close button. Before you close an application, make sure that you have saved any work you have done, otherwise you risk losing it. Fortunately, the computer usually reminds you if you have forgotten to do this before shutting the application down.

There is another method of altering the size of a window, which allows you to choose its size. Make sure the window is not completely filling the screen, and then place the pointer at any of the four corners of the window. The pointer will change from a broad arrowhead to a smaller double-headed arrow. By holding down the left mouse button you can now drag the pointer diagonally up or down to alter the size of the window to the size that suits you.

Ribbon tabs

This is the second bar from the top and consists of a number of options such as Home, Share and View (see Figure 4.3). By clicking on any of these tabs you will display a different toolbar offering a variety of different commands. The File tab works slightly differently in that it produces a dropdown menu offering access to previously used folders and files.

Figure 4.3

Click on the various tabs to see the effect on the contents of the different toolbar ribbons. You can always return to the original screen by tapping or clicking on the Home tab.

Viewing folders

It is possible that the screen shown in Figure 4.1 does not look like the one on your computer. To change the way your screen looks, click or tap on the View tab and choose Tiles. The content of any folder can be displayed as a list, a detailed list, icons of different sizes or tiles. Click on the Tiles option to display the window in the form shown in Figure 4.1. You can change the display size of the icons by choosing one of the icon size options. The list and detailed list views show the contents as folder names with greater or less detail, depending on the option you select.

With the View tab selected, click on the various options to see the different views available to you, before returning to the Tile view. Finish this exercise by returning to the Home tab.

Help button

This lies at the right end of the ribbon tab bar. Clicking on this icon raises a context-sensitive Help menu. We will be discussing the computer help facility in Chapter 9.

Toolbar ribbon

You'll notice that many of the command icons on the various ribbons in Figure 4.1 are 'greyed out'. This is where the icon is light grey rather than black, as it usually is. When an icon is greyed out, it indicates that the feature is not currently available.

Most of the icons on the ribbon are labelled but you can get more information about the action of any icon by placing the pointer on the icon; after a couple of seconds, a small text box will appear describing the action of the icon. Figure 4.4 shows the description of the Delete icon.

Figure 4.4

You will find this technique particularly valuable when using applications with toolbar icons that are too small to allow a descriptive label.

Breadcrumb bar

This lies immediately below the toolbar ribbon and displays a history of where you are in your navigation of the windows system. In Figure 4.1, this bar only shows Libraries as we have not yet moved away from this point.

Navigation buttons

These buttons (on the left of the breadcrumb bar) allow you to move back and forth between previously visited windows. They really come into their own when you are navigating your way through browser windows on the Internet but we will revisit those in Chapter 12.

Search box

By typing in a search word into this box (on the right of the breadcrumb bar) the computer will display all the occurrences of that word in the folders and files contained in the active window. We would not recommend using this feature at this stage as it would search the contents of all the libraries and result in a very long list — a time-consuming process! The Search box is much more useful when used in a specific folder.

Side bar

This is the column on the left side of the window, which displays the contents of the computer. The Favorites section shows frequently used folders and files. The Libraries section is divided into four folders: Documents, Music, Pictures and Videos. These are the storage areas for your relevant folders and files.

Because Libraries is the window displayed in Figure 4.1, the four folders in Libraries are shown as icons in the main part of the screen, as well as in the side bar.

You can safely ignore the Homegroup section at this stage. It is used to share access with a network of other printers and computers. A network is a group of interconnected devices and is beyond the scope of this book.

The section headed Computer shows the various components of the computer, such as the hard discs, DVD player and any other devices that are plugged into the computer (see Figure 4.5).

Figure 4.5

Opening a window

Let us progress from the basic window in Figure 4.1 to give you some practice at opening another window. Tap and hold or double-click on the icon for the Pictures folder in the main part of the screen. It is unlikely that you will have loaded any of your personal photos into this folder yet but your computer may have come with a few sample pictures installed. If so, you should see a folder labelled Sample Pictures. Double-click on this folder to reveal the image files.

Take a look at the breadcrumb bar in Figure 4.6. It displays the 'route' you have taken to arrive at the Sample Pictures folder. You can retrace your steps in two ways: click or tap on the words in the breadcrumb bar, or use the left navigation button. We will be discussing navigation in Chapter 5.

Figure 4.6

Live dangerously and double-click on one of the files in the Sample Pictures file to open the full picture on the screen. To close the picture, tap or click on the X symbol in the top-left corner.

The main window

This forms the largest part of the window screen and shows the contents of the selected folder. We will explore further features of a window in Chapter 8 when we show you how to open a simple Desktop application.

Summary

- Get to recognise the structure of a window. You may be using windows throughout your computing life.

- Use the Title bar to move the window around the screen.

- Use the ribbon tabs to show the various toolbars.

- The side bar offers useful links to other parts of the computer.

- Hovering the mouse pointer over an icon displays the function of that icon.

- The breadcrumb bar shows the route you have taken to arrive at the current screen.

- The navigation buttons remember where you have been recently and offer the opportunity to backtrack your movements.

- The Help button is found on many windows and is context-sensitive in that the information will refer to the application being used.

- Use the Search box to find files within a folder.

Brain training

Remember that there may be more than one correct answer to the following questions.

1. What is the function of the bread-crumb bar?

a) To help you navigate your way through the system

b) To collect items created by a technical process called a Computer Loaf

c) It shows you where you are in relation to other parts of the file system

d) It is a feature only used by computer engineers

2. Where are the sizing buttons?

a) On the taskbar

b) In the side panel

c) At the top-right corner of the screen

d) On a tape measure

3. What use is the side bar?

a) Not a lot

b) To access other parts of the computer system

c) To save time

d) It is of no use unless it has been activated

4. What will the Search box find?

a) Your car keys

b) A word in an open document

c) A long lost relative

d) A file listed in a window

Answers

Q1 – a and c   **Q2** – c

Q3 – b and c   **Q4** – d

PART II
Digging Deeper

You must have clicked on Vladivostok, instead of Venice.

Navigating the system

5

Equipment needed: A computer (laptop, tablet or desktop), Windows 8 operating system, monitor screen, preferably with touchscreen capability, keyboard and mouse or trackpad.

Skills needed: Keyboard and mouse (Chapter 1), knowledge of the Desktop interface (Chapter 3) and familiarity with windows (Chapter 4).

A computer contains one or more hard disks that hold a huge range of programs, folders and files. Many programs are used in the background to make sure that the computer operates correctly. For our purposes, the main program is the Windows 8 operating system. Other programs, applications or apps are controlled by you, and create folders and files. We have mentioned files and folders in previous chapters so now is the time to explain their functions in more detail.

The Windows 8 file system can be compared to a filing cabinet. The cabinet is the hard disk, while the drawers are the Libraries.

Disks, drives and memory

Computing beginners and even those who have been using computers for some time often confuse these three terms.

Disks

Most computers have one or more hard disks. These lie within the body of the computer and are referred to as internal disks. They are the storage warehouses for the operating programs and the files created by the user. External disks are small boxes that can be connected to the main computer by cables. They are used for long-term storage of folders and files, and to free up space on the internal hard disks. Data, which is the generic term for files, can also be stored on DVDs and memory sticks, which are simply other forms of external data storage.

Drives

Drives are often synonymous with disks, in that the first hard disk is often referred to as Drive C. (We need not go into the reason why it is labelled 'C' — it is related to the historical development of the home computer.) Drives also include other devices either permanently or temporarily connected to the computer. The DVD player found on most computers today is also a 'drive'. If you plug in a memory stick or camera card, they, too, are allocated a letter for identification purposes.

Figure 5.1 shows the contents of my computer. The computer has two hard disks (C and D), a DVD player drive (E) and a storage device drive (F), as well as a removable memory stick, labelled Kingston (G).

Memory

Memory comes in two forms — temporary and permanent. When you are typing a letter on the computer the information is stored in the temporary memory. If the power to the computer suddenly fails for some reason, all your hard work will disappear as if it had never existed. Permanent memory is provided by the hard disk. Only after you have saved your work to the hard disk is it safely retained. We will discuss saving your work later in the chapter. People often ask "How much memory have you got on your computer?" What they mean is "How much hard disk space have you got?"

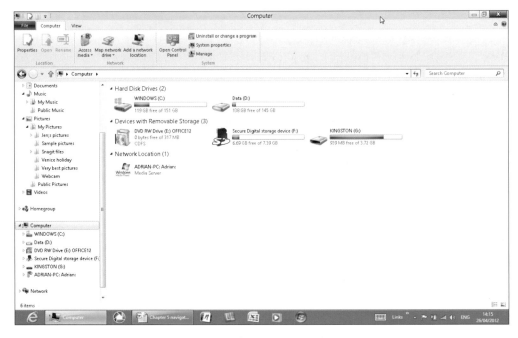

Figure 5.1

Available space

To find out how much free space is available on a disk, right-click on the name of the drive in the side bar and choose Properties from the dropdown menu. A pie chart will appear like the one in Figure 5.2, in which the available space in the Windows (C) disk is shown in magenta. Close this window by clicking on OK or the red X button in the top-right corner.

Libraries

There are normally four libraries — Documents, Pictures, Music and Videos. The Library 'drawers' contain folders and files. Folders simply contain subfolders and files. A file may be a document, photo, video or piece of music. You do not have to store your files in the named folder. For example, instead of saving your photo files in the Pictures library, you could save them in the Documents library in association with other document files if it suits your purpose, but it will be easier to find files if they are stored logically.

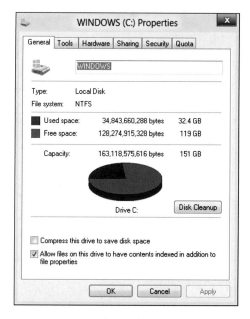

Figure 5.2

Folders

A Library, like the filing cabinet drawer, may contain several folders that, in turn, may contain further subfolders as well as individual files. Folders, and the files they contain, are more easily found if you have created a logical filing system. Your office filing cabinet may have a drawer for household information, which holds folders relating to your financial affairs, household repairs, council tax, utility bills and memorabilia. The financial folder may contain further folders devoted to correspondence with your bank, building society and tax returns. The bank folder will hold letters to and from the bank, while the electricity bill will go in the utilities folder. You can create as many folders as you like.

Creating new folders

You can open up the Libraries in one of two ways. From the Start screen, tap or click on the Windows Explorer tile. Do not confuse this with the Internet Explorer tile. They may have similar names but they perform very different functions. If you are using the Desktop screen, tap or click on the Libraries icon towards the left of the taskbar running along the bottom of the screen.

Either action will display the Libraries window that we discussed in Chapter 4. Double-click or tap on the Documents icon to open the Documents folder.

If you have a new computer the chances are that the Documents folder is completely empty of folders. To create a new folder, tap or click on the New Folder icon on the Home toolbar ribbon (see Figure 5.3).

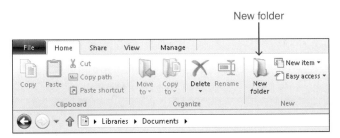

Figure 5.3

A new icon will appear on the screen with the title 'New folder' highlighted in blue. There is no point in having folders simply named 'New folder' so you need to give it a name that describes what you are going to keep in it. If the name is highlighted, as in Figure 5.4, the words will immediately be replaced when you start typing the new title. Type in the word 'Letters' and either hit the Enter key or click away from the icon. Congratulations! You have just created your first new folder. If you make a mistake while you are typing, just click on the folder, then click the right mouse button and select Rename from the dropdown menu that appears. The title of the folder will again be highlighted, allowing you to alter the text.

Figure 5.4

Now double-click on the Letters folders to open it. Click or tap on the New Folder icon again to create another folder and name the new file 'Family'.

Open the Pictures library and create a new folder named Holidays. Open that new folder and create another folder within in it, named Greece or Cruises.

Deleting folders

A folder may become redundant after a while and you may wish to remove it. There are two simple ways of doing this: either click or tap on the folder icon and hit the Delete key, or right-click on the icon and select Delete from the dropdown menu that appears.

If you delete a folder, you will also delete all the files contained within that folder. Before committing yourself to deleting a folder, take a moment to think, and check that there are no files within that folder that you want to keep. When you delete a folder or file it is automatically moved to the Recycle bin, from which you can restore it to your computer but it is unwise to rely too heavily on this safety net.

Files

Music applications create sound files; word processing applications create document files (such as letters, recipes, reports or advertising posters); and photographic applications create image files.

Let us take an example. You may have taken a photograph of your holiday in Greece. When you transfer the pictures of your Greek holiday to the computer, you will be asked which folder you would like the images to be saved in. You will be given the option to 'browse' the computer to locate an appropriate folder. Let's assume you have previously created a folder in your Pictures library called Holidays, within which you have created a folder called Greece. Click on the Browse button and navigate your way to the Greece folder (within the Holidays folder, which, in turn, lies in the Pictures library). Select this folder, and this is where your pictures will be stored.

Moving files

There will be occasions when you want to move files and folders to a different location. This involves dragging and dropping — holding the left mouse button down while dragging the item to a new location. If you only have access to a touchscreen, tap and hold your finger on the item and then drag the file with a finger to its new position.

Let us look at an example of how this is done. Figure 5.5 shows a folder called Venice Holiday, and the picture files stored in it. Let us say that you want to move one of these files to another Pictures folder you have created, called Very Best Pictures, which you can see in the folder list in the side bar. To do this, click on the file you want to move (which will cause it to become highlighted in blue, like Roofs of Venice in Figure 5.5), then drag the file across the screen to the sidebar and down to the Very Best Pictures folder. When the pointer is in the right place, the folder will light up in blue. Drop the file into the folder by releasing the mouse button or lifting your finger. Click or tap on the destination folder and you will see the file in the new folder.

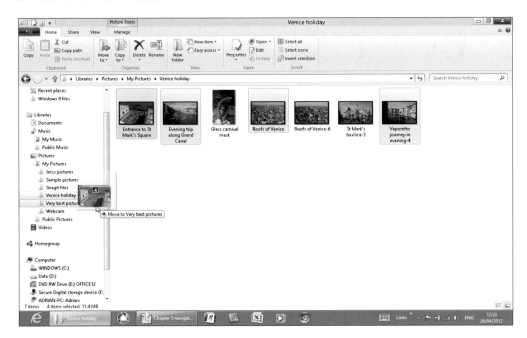

Figure 5.5

You do not have to move files one by one. You can move multiple files with similar ease. First of all you need to 'select' the files in question.

Selecting files

You can select files in one of two ways. If the files are next to each other, select them by clicking on the first file, moving the pointer to the last file, then holding down the Shift key before clicking on the last file. This will select both files and all the files in between them. Your target files may not be in a convenient, continuous order, however; to select these, hold down the Ctrl key while left-clicking on each file you want to select. You can also use the Ctrl+click function to select unwanted files from a continuous list, then remove them with a single click in the same way as you delete folders.

In Figure 5.6, four of the Venice pictures have been selected. To move them to a new folder, simply place the pointer over one of the selected files and drag it to the new folder in the sidebar. All the selected files will move with the dragged file.

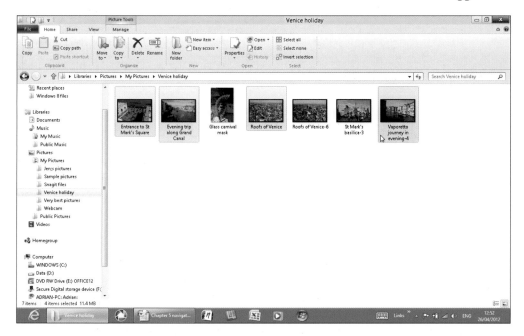

Figure 5.6

Copying files

When you move files, you simply transfer them from one folder to another — but you may want to have copies of the same file in more than one folder. In the previous example, you might like to have a copy of your Greek holiday photo in both the Greece and Very Best Pictures folders. To do this, you need to 'copy' the file rather than 'move' it. To copy a file, right-click on the file icon and choose Copy from the dropdown menu that appears. This will place a copy of the file in a temporary memory called the Clipboard. To place this copy into a different folder, open the folder in question, place the pointer anywhere in the main part of the window, right-click again and choose Paste from the dropdown menu. The copied file icon will immediately appear in the list of icons in the new folder.

Renaming files

Many files may have names that aren't particularly helpful. For example, image files from digital cameras are automatically given alphanumeric filenames by the camera, such as DSC156097, which is completely useless if you want to find a particular photo. It is easy to change the name of a folder or file. Navigate your way to the file or folder in question and right-click on it. The resulting dropdown menu offers the option of Renaming the item. Once the old name is highlighted, type in the new name and hit the Enter key.

Saving files

Every time you create a new file or alter an old one, you need to save it to the permanent memory of the computer. We explained the difference between temporary and permanent memory at the beginning of this chapter. You will find the Save option under the File button at the top left of the window.

To save a file, first navigate to the correct folder using the same navigation techniques we described earlier. Tap or click on the folder in which you want to save the file, then tap or click on the file to highlight its name, type in an appropriate name and click on Save. You will be offered a menu similar to the one in Figure 5.7. If you can't see your desired folder, navigate to it using the breadcrumb bar or the Up button, which takes you to a higher level in the folder 'tree'. You need not worry too much about this at the moment. It is the principle of navigating the filing system that we need to explain at this point. We will discuss the question of saving files in more detail in Chapter 8.

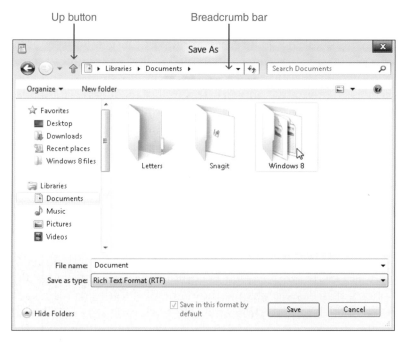

Figure 5.7

If you have opened a saved file and altered it (for example, by changing the text of a document or altering a picture in some way), saving the file will automatically replace the original file with the altered version without offering the Save menu. (Chapter 8 provides more detail on the importance for saving.)

Get into the habit of saving your work as you go along. There is nothing more frustrating than losing hours of work because you haven't used the Save command regularly.

Saving As

You may sometimes want to keep the original file as well as the altered version. For instance, you may have created a letterhead file to use when typing letters. You have opened the letterhead file and added text to create a letter. If you clicked on Save, you would overwrite the letterhead file with the text of the letter and your basic letterhead file would be lost. In this case, you want to retain the letterhead file for future use and create a new file containing the letter you have just written. To achieve this, instead of using the Save command, use the Save As command, which allows you to save the letter file as a separate file.

When you Save As, remember to use a different name for the new file — if you don't, you could still overwrite the original file.

Summary

- Disks contain programs, folders and files. They may be internal or external.

- Drives are almost synonymous with disks but include other storage devices such as DVDs, memory sticks and digital camera memory cards.

- In computing terms, memory can be temporary or permanent. Temporary memory is lost when the computer is turned off.

- Libraries contain folders that contain subfolders and files.

- Use the breadcrumb bar and navigation buttons to weave your way through the computer's folder 'tree'.

- You can create and delete as many folders as you like.

- You can have as many levels, or layers, of folders as you wish.

- Files can be moved, copied, saved and named.

- The Clipboard temporarily holds data that you have copied.

- The Save command creates a new file or overwrites an existing file that has been altered. The Save As command always creates a new file.

- Get into the habit of saving your work on a regular basis.

Brain training

There may be more than one correct answer to the following questions.

1. What is a hard disk?

   a) A DVD

   b) The operating system of the computer

   c) A very large storage device

   d) A digital camera memory card

2. What is temporary memory?

   a) Memory only held for a few minutes

   b) Data only held by the computer while the power is on

   c) Data that you are likely to forget

   d) Memory held on the Clipboard

3. What will you find in a folder?

   a) Other folders

   b) Data files

   c) Program files

   d) Printer files

4. What is the difference between the Save and Save As commands?

   a) There is none — they are both the same

   b) Save As allows you to create a new file

   c) Save creates a file in the temporary memory

   d) Save overwrites an original file

Answers

Q1 – c

Q3 – a, b and c

Q2 – b and d

Q4 – b and d

Customising the computer

6

Equipment needed: A computer (laptop, tablet or desktop), Windows 8 operating system, monitor screen, preferably with touchscreen capability, keyboard and mouse or trackpad.

Skills needed: Keyboard and mouse (Chapter 1), knowledge of the Desktop interface (Chapter 3) and familiarity with Windows (Chapter 4).

We discussed how to customise the Desktop screen in Chapters 2 and 3, which alters the appearance of the screen. There are many other ways to change the settings to suit your taste. Windows 8 offers so many customisation facilities that it is impossible to cover them all here, but in this chapter we will concentrate on the most useful options.

The Settings menu

The Settings menu will be familiar to you from Chapter 2. Raise the Charms menu by swiping from the right edge of the screen or placing the pointer at the top-right corner of the screen. Click or tap on Settings to raise the basic menu in Figure 6.1, which allows you to alter the volume, screen brightness and keyboard settings, and to turn the computer off. To access a wider range of options, tap or click on Change PC Settings.

Figure 6.1

As you can see (see Figure 6.2), the PC Settings menu offers a huge range of options in the left column so we are going to concentrate on the settings that will probably be most useful to you. Note that many of the menus accessed here are activated by tapping or clicking On/Off buttons.

Personalize

The Personalize section (see Figure 6.2) allows you to alter the appearance of the Lock and Start screens and add a picture of yourself to appear beside your account. To alter any of these pictures, choose the picture you want to replace it with, either by tapping or clicking on the image, or by clicking on the Browse button to be taken to your Pictures app, from which you can select an image of your choice.

Users

This section allows you to change your system password and other security measures to prevent unauthorised use of the computer. A good password should be sufficient for you at this stage but you can add the other measures later if required. You can also add more users with their own passwords, allowing each person to enjoy their own display preferences.

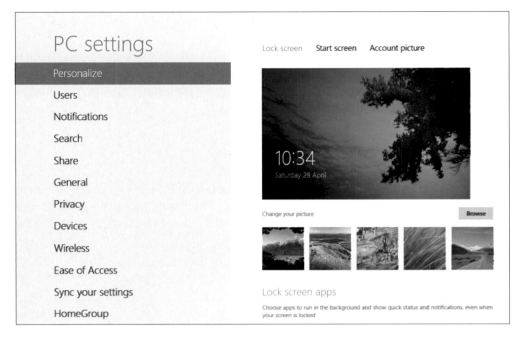

Figure 6.2

Notifications

Apps are continually being updated. In this section, you can choose whether to allow these updates or ignore them. Notifications of alterations to apps can be displayed on the Lock screen. You can even set the computer to make a particular sound to alert you of a new notification. The normal setting for these notifications is On, so you don't have to do anything at this stage unless you want to disable them.

Search

This allows you to instruct the computer to remember previous searches and select the apps you want to be included in a search. We suggest that you leave all of these switched to On for the time being.

Share

This allows you to decide which apps you want to use to share items like photos with other people. It can also be set to display information about previous sharing activities. Once again, the default setting is On. At this stage we would suggest turning this option off.

General

The largest set of options on the PC Settings page is under the General menu (see Figure 6.3), from which you can change many of the basic functions of the computer. The menu is too long for all the options to be onscreen at once, so scroll the screen upwards to access them all.

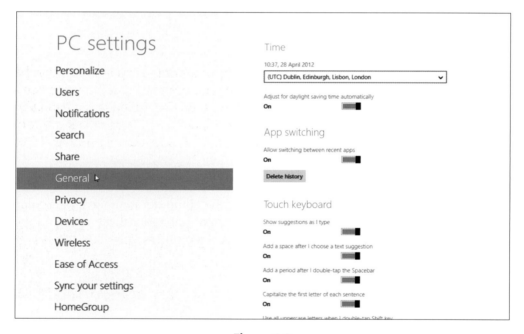

Figure 6.3

The General menu is used to do things like changing the time zone, controlling the method of switching between apps, clearing the history of your app use from the computer, setting up various touchscreen functions, refreshing the computer and resetting the computer to its original state.

Touch keyboard

There is a lot you can do to personalise the touchscreen functions, so experiment as much as you like. For example, you can set the spelling section to correct mis-spellings, ask it to capitalise the first letter of new sentences automatically or turnkey sounds on and off. If you are working in a different language, you can even download and install a keyboard for that language from this menu.

Refresh

If you have made a complete mess of personalising your settings or the computer is beginning to run slowly, you can tidy things up by using the Refresh facility. Use this setting with care and follow the instructions to avoid losing any apps you have downloaded.

Reset

Security is always a problem when you get rid of an old computer — it can be quite difficult to be sure you have removed all your personal data from the computer before giving it to someone else. Windows 8 offers a quick and clean solution to this problem in the form of the Reset option, which removes all your personal files and restores the computer to its original state ('factory settings'). We discuss security in more detail in Chapter 11.

Do not use the Reset option unless you are absolutely sure you want to remove all your personal files, photos and music forever! It is a wise precaution to 'back up' these files by copying them to an external hard disk before you reset your computer.

Privacy

This option is not as comprehensive as it may seem, and refers only to what you are prepared to allow apps to do with your information (such as use your location, name and picture). You need to be careful how much information you give away to others so, although the normal settings are set to On, you may wish to change some of them. Further privacy settings can be accessed from the Control Panel, which we will deal with in a minute.

Devices

This option is used when you add some external devices, such as printers, and is probably best left to your guardian angel for now. You do not need to use it for all external devices — for example, cameras are recognised automatically when you plug them into the computer, so you don't need to use this option.

Wireless

Use this to turn the wireless (Wi-Fi) connection on and off. There is also a Flight mode, which prevents any wireless signals from interfering with other networks such as in an aircraft or hospital.

Ease of access

This is designed for users with sight and hearing difficulties. You can change the brightness of the screen and even get the computer to convert text to speech using the Narrator function.

Sync your settings

This is another rather advanced feature of Windows 8. It allows you to share your settings with other computers using the Windows Live applications. We will be discussing the download and use of this feature in Chapter 12. You can safely ignore this option for now.

HomeGroup

This is another advanced setting that allows the sharing of information between other computers, and is an area that is best left to your guardian angel.

Windows update

This notifies you of any recent updates to the Windows 8 operating system.

Control Panel

To access the Control Panel make sure that you first touch the Desktop tile and then, when the desktop is visible on the screen, access the Charms menu as before. The Control Panel will now be one of the options. The Control Panel will be more familiar to you if you have used previous Windows operating systems.

As you can see in Figure 6.4, the layout of the Control Panel offers many of the options afforded by the Settings menu.

Figure 6.4

Power settings

You can save battery life by altering the length of time before the computer goes into Sleep mode. You can also change what happens when you close the lid of a laptop or activate the power button. You have the option to turn the computer off, send it into Sleep mode or send it into Hibernation mode. The easiest way to do this is to activate a search for the word 'power'. With the Start screen showing, type the word "power", click on Settings and choose the option you require.

Sleep and Hibernation

Sleep is a power-saving state that allows a computer to quickly resume full-power operation (typically within several seconds) when you want to start working again. Putting your computer into the Sleep state is like pausing a DVD player — the computer immediately stops what it's doing and is ready to start again when you want to resume working.

Hibernation is a power-saving state designed primarily for laptops. While Sleep puts your work and settings in memory and draws a small amount of power, Hibernation puts your open documents and programs on your hard disk, and then turns off your computer. Of all the power-saving states in Windows, hibernation uses the least amount of power. On a laptop, use hibernation when you know that you won't be using your laptop for while and won't have an opportunity to charge the battery during that time.

Searching the computer for apps, settings and files

Windows 8 provides a very efficient search facility. The system will search for any word that appears in your Apps, Settings and Files.

Searching from the Desktop

The Control Panel has a search box in the top-right corner of the window (see Figure 6.4). Place the cursor in the box by tapping or clicking in the box, and type in a search word. Almost immediately, you will be presented with a list of Control Panel subjects that relate to your search word. Click on the subject that you want to alter.

Searching from the Start screen

The search facility offered by Windows 8 is faster and more comprehensive than previous Windows systems. There is no search box on the Start screen itself but there are two ways to search the computer for information from here: either raise the Charms menu and select Search or simply start typing on the Start screen.

For instance, you may want to find out how to add a new user to your computer. Typing the word "user" on the Start screen results in a list of Apps, Settings and Files that involve the word, as shown in Figure 6.5. In this case, you'll see in the right column that the search has found no relevant apps but that 17 settings and more than 2,000 files contain the word "user". In Figure 6.5, the Settings category has been selected (by tapping or clicking) to reveal the options. The list of settings is too long to fit onto a single screen, so you need to swipe the screen from right to left to view the rest of the list.

Figure 6.5

Try to use a word that focuses on what you are searching for. If you had searched for the word "add" rather than "user", for example, you would have found 80 settings. Searching for "add user", however, would have narrowed the search down to just 8 settings.

It is easier to find photos if you have given them a descriptive file name rather than leaving the alphanumeric file name allocated by the camera. Chapter 5 describes how to rename files.

Changing the pointer settings

You can alter the size, shape, speed and sensitivity of the mouse pointer by doing a search on the Start screen. Type in "pointer" and click on Settings, where you will find an option to Change how the Mouse Pointer Looks (among other options). Click on this icon to display the menu (see Figure 6.6).

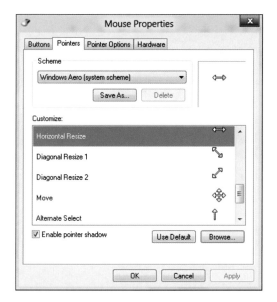

Figure 6.6

Select the pointer you want to change and then tap or click on Browse to view other options. Select the pointer of your choice and tap or click on Apply to change the appearance.

Summary

- By adding users, each person can have their own preferred computer settings.

- Play around with your computer settings to see what suits you.

- Use the Settings option from the Start screen, or use the Control Panel from the Desktop view.

- Don't forget that you can alter the appearance of the Desktop screen by using the right-click function.

- You can set up your computer to accommodate impaired sight and hearing.

- The Hibernation mode uses far less battery power than the Sleep mode.

- Use the Start screen search facility to find apps, applications, settings and files.

- Labelling files with accurate names improves the Search results.

Brain training

There may be more than one answer to the following questions.

1. How would you change the settings on the computer?

a) Use the Settings option from the Charms menu

b) Use the Control Panel

c) Search for a word relevant to the change you wish to make

d) Right-click on the Desktop screen

2. How would you change the computer's password?

a) You can't — once the password has been set, it is locked in

b) Return it to the supplier

c) Search for the word 'password' on the Start screen

d) Use the Control Panel search box

3. What is the difference between the Sleep and Hibernation modes?

a) The computer takes longer to open from Sleep mode

b) Hibernation saves battery life more efficiently

c) Sleep is used by desktops and laptops, while Hibernation is a feature of tablet computers

d) The differences are only technical

4. How does Refresh differ from Reset?

a) Refresh recharges the battery

b) Refresh tidies up the computer

c) Reset closes all the open applications

d) Reset wipes all your personal data from the computer

Answers

Q1 – a, b and c

Q2 – c and d

Q3 – b

Q4 – b and d

Opening your first app

Equipment needed: A computer (laptop, tablet or desktop), Windows 8 operating system, monitor screen, preferably with touchscreen capability, keyboard and mouse or trackpad.

Skills needed: Keyboard and mouse (Chapter 1), knowledge of the Desktop screen (Chapter 3) and familiarity with Windows (Chapter 4).

So far we have been dealing with the basics — essential but a little dry. Now we are going to put the computer to practical use. As you have seen, the Start screen is full of tiles, which are shortcuts to the apps and larger applications on the machine. Your computer will already have many of the basic apps loaded onto it by the manufacturer, and we are going to use some of these in this chapter. There is more advanced information about apps in Chapter 14 but for now we are going to look at three relatively simple apps — Solitaire (the patience card game), Paint (a drawing program) and Maps. The first two will introduce you to the basic use of the mouse pointer and touch gestures, while Maps will show you what a larger app is capable of.

The Solitaire app

Solitaire has always been old favourite with Microsoft Windows. It is still available in Windows 8 but rather than coming pre-installed with Windows you now have to fetch it from the Windows store. This is a fairly straightforward process.

From the Windows Start screen, type Solitaire into the search box and then select the Store tile from the menu. You now see nine apps, as shown in Figure 7.1. You can choose from the simple to the collection. In this case, select the Simple Solitaire and then click install. Once installed, you will see a tile on the Start screen. Tap or click on it to start the game.

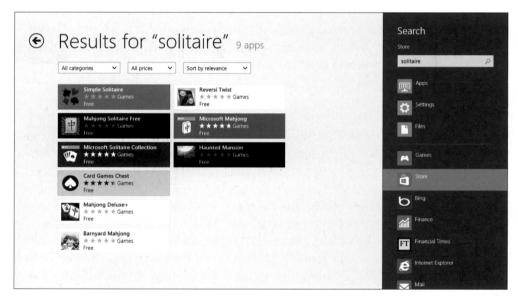

Figure 7.1

Figure 7.2 shows the start of a Solitaire game. It is a version of the old patience game we used to play as children — before the advent of shoot 'em up computer games. As you can see, the eight of hearts can be moved onto the nine of clubs. Do this by dragging the card, using a finger or the mouse. The card then drops into place and the next card in the column is automatically turned over. Just as in patience, kings can be moved into open columns, while aces and their suit cards can be added to the four blocks above the card layout. If you wish to reverse an action, tap or click on the Undo icon in the bottom left-corner.

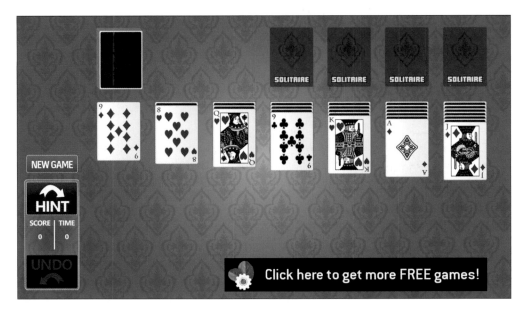

Figure 7.2

It is a very simple game but it will give you valuable practice in the use of mouse click commands and touchscreen gestures. If you are stuck or want to start a new game, right-click on the screen or touch the screen with your finger and keep it pressed for a few seconds. A menu will appear at the bottom of the screen offering you the option to receive a hint about your next move or start a new game.

If you have the sound turned on you will hear the sound of the cards being dealt and moved. These are quite realistic but may begin to get on your nerves. To turn off the sound, just go to the Charms menu, click or tap on the volume icon and drag the slider to the bottom. Alternatively, if your keyboard has volume buttons, pressing those will show the slider on the screen and you can adjust the volume accordingly.

Closing an app

Close an app at any time by dragging the pointer or a finger sharply down from the top edge of the screen. You may have to attempt this several times before you get the hang of it but practice makes perfect. All open apps close when the computer is shut down, unless there is an action that needs to be completed. For instance, if you have been creating a document and try to shut the computer down before saving your work, a message will appear to tell you to save the document before shutting the computer down. Cancel the shut down, return to the app and complete the required action before issuing another shut down command.

For our purposes, do not close the Solitaire app just yet but return to the Start screen by hitting the Start button or pointing to the lower-right of the screen and tapping. You'll find out why later in the chapter.

The Paint app

Find the Paint tile (see Figure 7.3) on the Start screen or the list of All Apps, and click on it.

Figure 7.3

Paint is a simple drawing application that runs in Desktop mode and therefore appears in a window with its now familiar structure (see Figure 7.4). To start drawing, tap or click on the Brushes icon to reveal the options.

Figure 7.5 shows the dropdown menu of the various brush options. Point at the small icons to see what action each brush performs. In this case, we have pointed at the top-right icon, which is identified as an airbrush. Click or tap on the brush type and then choose a colour by clicking or tapping on one of the colour squares on the toolbar (Figure 7.4). You are now ready to paint.

Drawing area   Tools

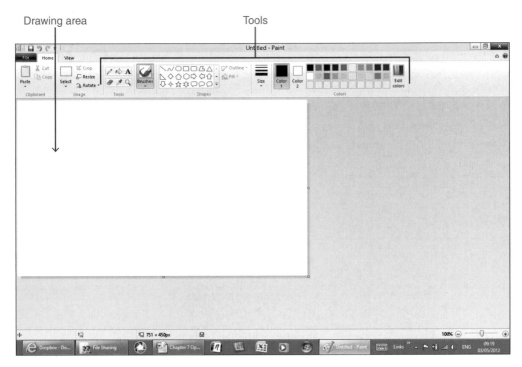

Figure 7.4

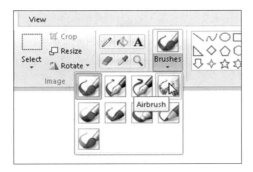

Figure 7.5

Drag the pointer or use a finger to draw your first line in the drawing area. Release the left mouse button or lift your finger from the screen to end the drawing stroke. Add further strokes to add to your masterpiece. You can change the brush size, type and colour at any time. If you make a mistake you can 'undo' a previous action: simply tap or click on the Undo icon on the Quicklaunch bar, or use Ctrl+Z.

Using the various tools (see Figure 7.6) you can add text to your drawing, erase any parts you are unhappy with and fill enclosed spaces with colour.

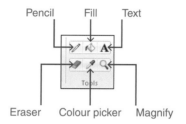

Figure 7.6

Figure 7.7 shows a 'doodle' we created using various brushes, colours, the Fill tool and Text option. You can use the Paint app simply for doodling or, more constructively, for making quick diagrams.

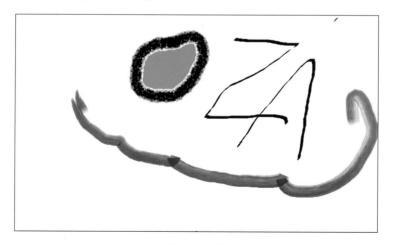

Figure 7.7

Give it a try. You probably won't create a masterpiece suitable for the Royal Academy's Summer Exhibition but you will gain valuable experience in using both mouse and touch commands. The important thing is to have fun while you learn.

 When you are using the Fill tool, make sure that the area you wish to fill with colour is completely enclosed otherwise you will fill the whole of the background.

Saving your drawings

You may want to save some drawings and discard others. To save a drawing, tap or click on the File tab and select Save from the dropdown menu; navigate your way to the folder of your choice; name the file and select OK. If you want to abandon your artistic efforts, click or tap on the red X icon on the sizing buttons at the top right of the window. You will be presented with a message asking you if you want to save the file (see Figure 7.8). Discard the file by selecting Don't Save. If you change your mind about closing the file, select Cancel.

In this case, once again, do not close the Paint app yet but return to the Start screen.

Figure 7.8

 If you do not save or discard the file and try to shut the computer down, you will be reminded that you have an unsaved file and the computer will not close. Cancel the shut down, return to the Paint app and save or discard the file before turning the machine off.

The Maps app

Maps, shown in Figure 7.9, is a genuinely new app designed for Windows 8 and uses a number of the new facilities offered by the new system. You will need to be connected to the Internet for this app to work properly.

Figure 7.9

This is a pre-installed app and will certainly be available on the Start screen. Click or tap on the Maps tile to open the app. If you do not see the Start screen, just tap the Windows key or point to the bottom-left corner of the screen and click on the screen image.

This is a much more comprehensive app than those we have looked at previously. When the app opens, it asks whether you wish to use your own location. If you have a laptop or tablet with the right SatNav technology and answer yes, a map will appear with a diamond hovering over your physical location (see Figure 7.10). The accuracy will depend upon how good the technology in your device is — in our case it is correct to within about 100 metres. If your computer does not have SatNav technology it will pick a location based upon where it thinks your computer is, which may be completely incorrect. The computer labels this "My Location". That can be annoying, but you can always drag the map to where you actually are. If the menu option at the bottom of the screen is not visible, right-click on the screen or touch the screen and keep your finger pressed until the menu appears.

My Location

No matter what map you are looking at, pressing the My Location button on the menu will always move the map back to where it thinks you are but remember this is not necessarily correct.

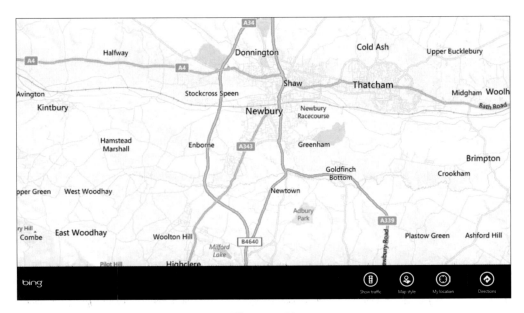

Figure 7.10

Sizing maps

The initial map may not be detailed enough for you, or may show too localised a view. This is easily changed by resizing or zooming the map. To zoom in or out, use pinch or stretch gestures on the screen. Place two fingers on the screen and either pinch them together or stretch them apart to alter the scale of the map. If you are restricted to the use of a mouse, the same effects can be achieved by clicking on the plus and minus buttons on the left side of the screen.

Moving maps

You can move the displayed map easily by dragging the pointer or a finger across the screen in the desired direction.

Displays

The Maps app does a lot more than displaying a map of roads. Try clicking on the Map Style button on the lower menu and choosing Aerial View to change the view to an aerial photographic display.

Traffic

This button on the lower menu gives information about current traffic conditions on the displayed map.

Directions

This is a particularly useful feature of the Maps app. Let us assume that you live in London and you have been invited to a family reunion at Stratton-on-the-Fosse in Somerset. You can use the Maps app to generate details of your proposed journey. Use the right mouse button to display the menu and then select Directions.

Enter your starting point (in this case, Agnes Road, London) in the from box (see Figure 7.11). Click on Directions, which is available on both the upper and lower menus. Click in the empty box and enter the destination address. If you need to alter the direction of travel, click or tap on the double arrow icon between the destinations.

Figure 7.11

Now click on Go and the computer will calculate the route and provide you with a detailed map, driving directions and an estimation of the journey time (see Figure 7.12).

As you can see from Figure 7.12, the estimated driving distance is 120 miles taking approximately 2 hours, 28 minutes. The route directions lie across the top of the map and can be scrolled from right to left to reveal further instructions.

As before, do not close the Maps app but return to the Start screen.

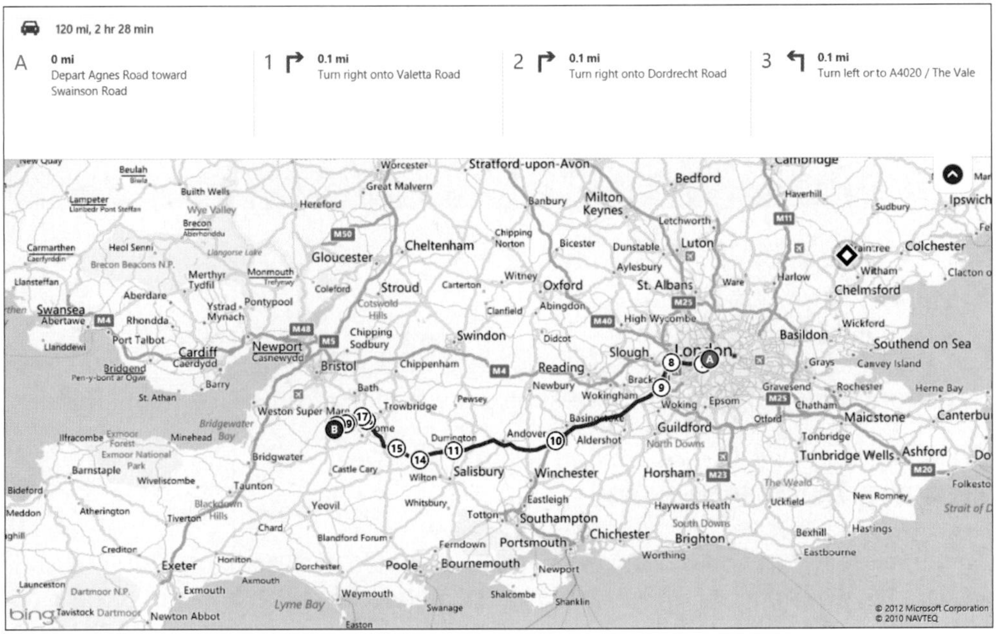

Figure 7.12

Searching Maps

The maps we have on our computer are a cut down version of the Microsoft Bing maps. If we use Internet Explore and go to www.bing.com we can select maps and search for locations. Follow the above instructions and you see a search box where you can type in the name of a place. Type a place name into the box to find its location. Click or tap the blue magnifying glass symbol to the right of the box. The map will change to reveal the location.

Try to make your search as specific as you can. If we had simply searched for `Shepton Mallett', we may have been taken to various Sheptons in the USA. It is good practice to separate parts of the address by commas. For instance, typing in `Church Street' is too vague; instead, type `Church Street, Boxted, Colchester' to get to the road in question.

The Maps app does not just find geographical sites -- you can use it to find businesses as well.

Type "Harrods" in the search box and you will be taken to a map showing the location of the famous London store.

Menus

If, at any time, you need to raise a menu, right-click on the screen or flick up from the bottom edge of the screen. Repeating either action removes the menu options.

Moving between apps

We have asked you not to close the apps you opened in this chapter for a reason. You can have as many as seven apps running at the same time. You can scroll back to the previous app by swiping from the left edge of the screen. Repeat this action to move through the open apps one at a time.

To view all the open apps, place the pointer at the top-right corner of the screen and then move it down the left edge to display small screenshots of the open apps. Click on the one you need, to display the app window.

Summary

- Apps may open in either Start or Desktop mode.

- To close an app, drag down the screen from top to bottom. This may take some practice.

- Open apps can be revealed by pointing at the top-right corner of the screen and moving the pointer down.

- A previous open app can be displayed by swiping from the left edge of the screen.

- All apps can be displayed by right-clicking on the Start screen or flicking up from the bottom edge.

- With All Apps displayed, an app can be pinned to the Start menu by using the right-click menu.

- Open app menus by right-clicking or flicking up from the bottom edge.

- All open apps will close when the computer is shut down.

- Enlarge an app screen by stretching two fingers away from each other on the screen or trackpad.

- Reduce an app screen by pinching two fingers together on the screen or trackpad.

- Some screens can be moved by dragging the pointer or finger across the screen.

- Save or discard your work before shutting the computer down.

Brain training

There may be more than one correct answer to the following questions.

1. What does a right-click do?

   a) Closes an app

   b) Opens the previously used app

   c) Raises a menu

   d) Displays the Charms menu

2. How would you enlarge a map?

   a) Use Ctrl and the plus key

   b) Use the stretch gesture

   c) Click or tap on the magnifying plus icon

   d) Swipe from any corner of the screen

3. How would you reverse an action?

   a) Use Ctrl+Z

   b) Use Ctrl+U

   c) Click or tap on the Undo icon

   d) Press the Esc key

4. How would you start a new Solitaire game?

   a) Close the app and start again

   b) Press Ctrl+N

   c) Swipe from the top of the screen

   d) Right-click and choose New Deal

Answers

Q1 – c

Q3 – a and c

Q2 – b and c

Q4 – d

Opening your first Desktop application

8

Equipment needed: A computer, Windows 8 operating system, keyboard and mouse or trackpad. A printer would be useful.

Skills needed: Keyboard and mouse (Chapter 1), Desktop screen (Chapter 3), windows (Chapter 4) and navigation (Chapter 5).

In this chapter, you are going to use a program, or application, for the first time. The application we have chosen is a basic word processing program found on all Windows 8 systems called WordPad. Word processing creates text in the form of a letter, report, poster or other document. You do not need to be able to touch type to use the keyboard.

Opening an application

To start the application you need to have the Start screen in view. (If it is not visible, tap the Windows key on the keyboard.) Your computer should have been set up so that the WordPad tile (see Figure 8.1) is towards the right end of the tiles. Swipe your finger or drag the mouse pointer from right to left across the touchscreen until the WordPad tile comes into view. Tap or click on the tile and the Start screen will be replaced by the WordPad window (see Figure 8.2). If the tile is not visible, right-click on the mouse and All Apps will appear. Click this and follow the previous procedure to locate WordPad.

Figure 8.1

If you cannot find WordPad on the screen, you can also use the Search facility on the Start screen. Type the word 'wordpad' and the application tile will appear. You can pin the tile to the Start screen for future use by right-clicking on the tile, or swiping a finger up from the bottom edge of the screen, and choosing the Pin To Start Menu option.

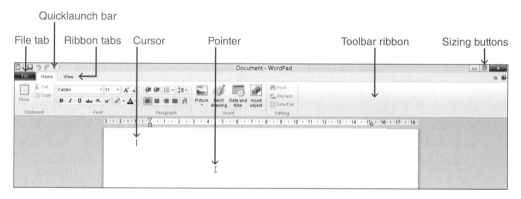

Figure 8.2

You should be able to recognise many of the basic features of the WordPad window from Chapter 4. The two main differences are the flashing vertical line towards the top-left corner of the white page area, and the toolbar ribbon. When the mouse pointer is over the white paper area, it also changes shape from an arrow to a curious capital I shape. This is known as an I-pointer and denotes that the pointer is within an area you can type into. If the I-pointer is not visible, click the mouse and it will appear.

Try typing a few words on the keyboard to see the effects on the screen. Use the space bar to separate the words and the Enter key to create new lines and paragraphs. Play around with it. At this stage, it does not matter what sort of a mess you make, you can always get rid of it. The important thing is to become familiar with the effects of keyboard strokes on the screen. You could try typing out the beginning of a story, copying a newspaper article or creating a letterhead. Try not to be too heavy-handed when pressing the keys. If you hold down a key for too long, the letter will be repeated at an alarming rate!

There are many ways to delete what you have written onscreen but, for now we want you to place the cursor at the very end of what you have typed. To do this, place the I-pointer at the end of the text and left-click. Then hold down the Backspace key until all the text has been removed. The Backspace key deletes all characters to the *left* of the cursor. You could place the cursor at the beginning of the text and hold down the Delete key, which removes the characters to the *right* of the cursor. You cannot place the cursor beyond the last typing point. If you want to extend the typing space, add extra lines by hitting the Enter key several times after the last typing entry.

To summarise, the cursor moves with the typing and the pointer is moved by the mouse. The pointer is used to place the cursor by clicking where you want to start typing.

As an exercise, we are going to create a letterhead that you can use when you write letters. Type in your address, using the Enter key to create new lines.

Selecting text

Your letterhead probably looks unimpressive so far, so you will want to modify it to suit your own taste. To do this, you must first select the text. Place the mouse pointer at the top- left corner of the letterhead text and drag the pointer across and down over the text. This will highlight the text in blue as shown in Figure 8.3. 'Selecting' will become a common tool in your typing arsenal. Once you have selected the text, you can begin to modify it to suit your needs.

Figure 8.3

You can change the appearance of the type by using various options on the toolbar ribbon (see Figure 8.4).

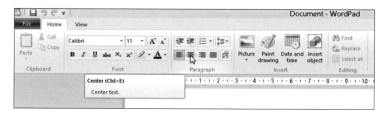

Figure 8.4

You may be confused by all the icons and symbols on this ribbon at first, but you can easily identify each icon by placing the mouse pointer over it — without clicking — and the action that icon performs will be displayed within a few seconds. In Figure 8.4, the pointer is over the icon that positions the text in the centre of the page if that icon is clicked.

Place the pointer over the symbols one by one and their actions will be displayed. By selecting the text and using the icons on the toolbar, you can change the alignment of the text, its colour and its size. You can also make the type bold, italic or underlined.

Formatting text

Look at the left end of the toolbar ribbon and you will see the name of the font that is being used for your text. In Figure 8.4, the font is Calibri. To the right of this is a box showing the figure 11, which tells you what size the font is. Click on the small arrow to the right of the box and a dropdown menu will offer different font sizes.

Click on 16 and watch the size of the letters increase. (You can see examples of dropdown menus in Figures 8.6 and 8.7.) Making sure your text is still selected, click on the B symbol at the left of the toolbar and the text will become emboldened. You can then centre the text by clicking on the icon shown in Figure 8.3. You can also align the text to the left or right, or have it justified, which 'stretches' the lines of type so there are no ragged edges in the right-hand margin. The underlined letter <u>A</u> allows you to alter the colour of the text.

When you use the formatting tools, remember that they will only affect text that you have selected.

Figure 8.5 shows the original letterhead changed to a font called Arial Black with the size increased to 16, centred and coloured red. Try it out for yourself and once you have finished you can remove the selection by clicking or tapping on any point away from the selected area.

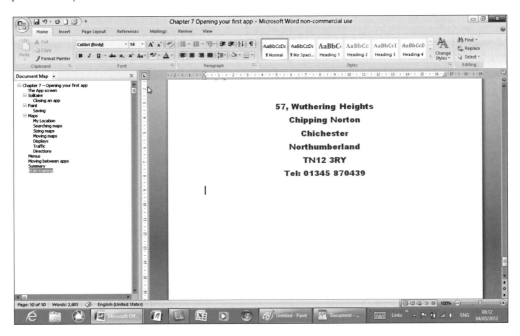

Figure 8.5

Dropdown menus

Any symbol with a small arrow to its right will produce a dropdown menu. Figures 8.6 and 8.7 show the dropdown menu for fonts.

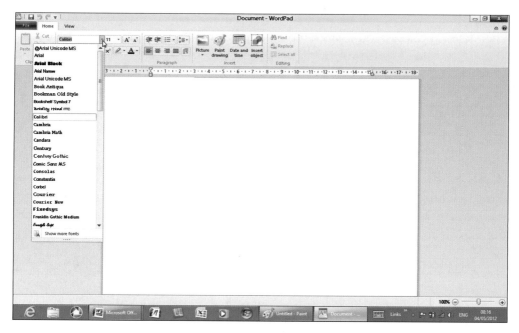

Figure 8.6

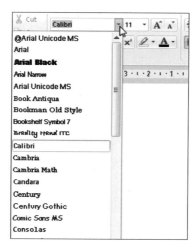

Figure 8.7

Figures 8.8 and 8.9 show the dropdown menu for text colour. To select the font or colour you want, simply left-click on the option on the menu.

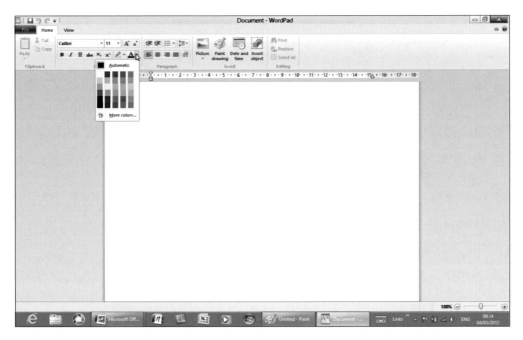

Figure 8.8

Figure 8.9

Further selection tips

So far we have only used the 'dragging' technique to select the type but there are other ways of selecting parts of a typed document.

- To select a single word, double left-click on the word.

- To select a line, move the pointer into the left margin. It will change from an I-pointer to a right-pointing arrow. Align the arrow opposite the line and left-click. You can select multiple lines by dragging the pointer arrow down the margin.

- To select a block of text, place the cursor at the beginning of the block then move the pointer to the end of the block, hold down the Shift key and left-click.

- To select a paragraph, triple-click anywhere within the paragraph text.

- To select the whole document, use the keyboard shortcut of Ctrl+A (in other words, hold down the Ctrl key while hitting the A key).

Deleting text

You have already deleted text by using the Backspace and Delete keys but there is a faster way of removing unwanted text. Simply select the text you want to delete and hit the Delete key and all the selected will be deleted. If you delete some text accidentally, reinstate it by using the Undo icon or Ctrl+Z.

Inserting text

To insert some new text into a document you have been working on, move the I-pointer to where you want the new text to go and left-click to place the cursor there. Anything you type will now be inserted at this point. If you want to return to typing at the end of the document, simply reposition the cursor at the end of the text.

The Quick Access bar

This is found on the title bar of the WordPad window, to the left of the document's file name (see Figure 8.10). It affords instant access to common actions such as saving, printing and creating new documents, thus bypassing the need to use the File menu.

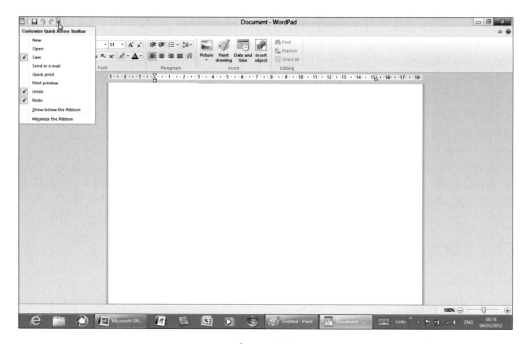

Figure 8.10

You can customise the range of actions displayed here by clicking on the small black arrow at the right of the bar (see Figure 8.11) and then clicking on the action you wish to include in the bar.

Figure 8.11

The Undo and Redo icons

The Quick Access bar also contains the Undo icon (the anticlockwise arrow in Figures 8.10 and 8.11). Many apps or applications allow you to cancel a previous action, for example when you have made a typing error, accidentally formatted something or inserted the wrong picture. As soon as you realise your mistake, hit the Undo icon to reverse the most recent action. If you have 'undone' an action and realised that it was no mistake after all, use the Redo icon (the clockwise arrow) to restore what you have undone. Some applications allow multiple Undo actions while others only store the last action. The keyboard shortcut to undo is Ctrl+Z and the Redo shortcut is Ctrl+Y.

The Backspace and Delete keys

You will inevitably make typing mistakes so you need to know how to correct them. Take a look at the example in Figure 8.12. You could delete the error-strewn text and type it again but that would be tedious and time-consuming and there are simpler ways to amend it.

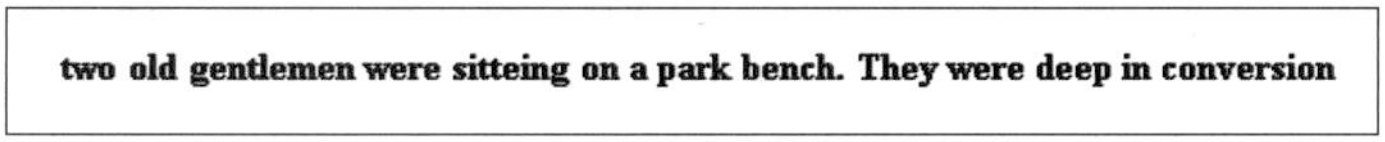

> two old gentlemen were sitteing on a park bench. They were deep in conversion

Figure 8.12

The first mistake is the missing capital letter at the beginning. Place the cursor at the beginning of the sentence, hit the Delete key and insert the capital T. To correct the spelling of 'sitting', place the cursor to the right of the 'e' by clicking the pointer at that position, and press the Backspace key to remove it. Finally, correct the spelling of 'conversation' by placing the cursor between the 'r' and the 't' and typing in the missing letters.

Beginners often find it difficult to place the cursor accurately with the mouse pointer. You can overcome this by placing the cursor close to where you want it to go and then manoeuvring it into the right position by using the arrow navigation keys on the keyboard to move it up, down or sideways, one space at a time.

Saving your work

Your first attempt at creating a text document will have been full of mistakes, corrections, alterations — and a certain amount of frustration. So, when you have finally achieved the finished article, the last thing you want is to lose all your hard work. This means saving your work to the permanent memory of the hard disk. Before you save it, the document is held in a temporary memory and will be lost when you shut down the computer.

In the top-left corner of the window, you will find the File tab, just to the left of the Home tab. Click on this icon to release a dropdown menu (Figure 8.13). This menu offers a number of options, including saving the document. Click on Save. This opens up the Documents window. The suggested filename will be 'Document', which is of little value, so replace this with a more descriptive name such as 'Letter to Mr Jones' or 'Letterhead'. In Chapter 5, you created a folder named Letters. You could navigate your way to this folder before saving the document so that the Letterhead file is saved in a folder that is relevant. This will allow you to find the document easily when you need to refer to it in the future.

Another useful feature of the File menu is that it lists recently opened files, allowing you to open them instantly by clicking on the file name. In Figure 8.13, there is only one Recent Document — Letter to Fred. This list will grow as you save more document files.

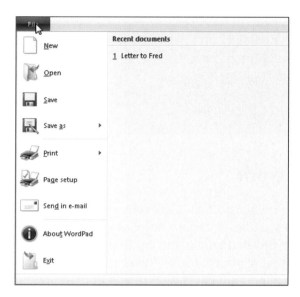

Figure 8.13

Creating a new folder

If you rely on saving all your documents in the Documents folder, the folder will start to become cluttered with documents ranging from letters to the bank, committee minutes and correspondence with family to details of your family history (see Figure 8.14). You can organise this clutter by creating folders to store your documents. Create a new folder by clicking on New Folder on the Home toolbar ribbon and replacing the suggested name of 'New Folder' with a name that describes contents (such as 'Family' or 'Finances', for example). You can then 'drag' individual files into their respective folders as explained in Chapter 5.

The File menu also offers the options to Print documents, Open files and create New documents. There is also an option to Save As, instead of the normal Save option. This can be confusing so we should sort it out once and for all.

Breadcrumb bar

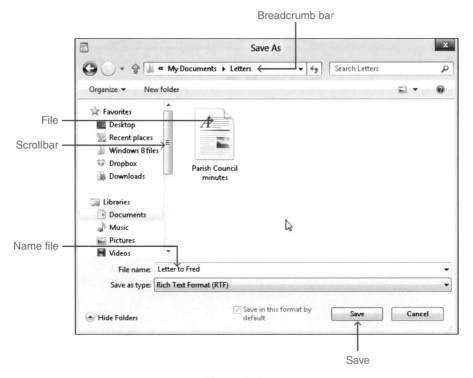

File

Scrollbar

Name file

Save

Figure 8.14

Let us assume that you want to use the file called Letterhead to compose a letter to Mr Jones, so you open the Letterhead file by choosing Open from the File menu, clicking on the Letterhead file and writing your letter to Mr Jones under the letterhead. If you then issued the Save command, this would overwrite the original Letterhead file with the contents of Mr Jones' letter. To retain the original Letterhead file, use the Save As command (Figure 8.13) to create a new file named Letter to Mr Jones, leaving the original Letterhead file unchanged.

Don't forget to save your work on a regular basis, especially before you close the application down — you don't want all your hard work to go down the plughole. Fortunately, WordPad and many other apps are quite forgiving in this situation. If it detects that you have not saved a document before closing, it will display a message asking you if you wish to save the work (see Figure 8.15). You will normally choose 'yes' unless you have been playing around with the application and have a complete mess on the screen. In this case, exit without saving and the mess will be consigned to the great dustbin in the sky.

Figure 8.15

Finding files

If you can't locate a file you can always find it again by using the Start screen search facility. To find the Letter to Mr Jones file, simply type 'jones' on the Start screen and it will appear under the Files heading. Open it by tapping or clicking on the file icon.

As this has probably been the first time you have opened an application (never-mind used the keyboard in earnest), this is a good place to stop and get your breath back. Save your work, close the application by clicking on the red X button at the top-right corner of the window and relax — make yourself a well-earned cup of tea or play a game of Solitaire.

WordPad is a very basic word processing application. There are many more advanced word processing applications, such as Microsoft Word and Open Office, but the basic principles outlined in this chapter are the same for all of them.

Summary

- The flashing cursor is where any typing will be inserted. The I-pointer moves with the mouse and is used to position the cursor.

- Use the space bar to separate the words and the Enter key to add new lines or paragraphs.

- The Backspace key deletes characters to the *left* of the cursor while the Delete key removes those to the *right*.

- To format text you have typed in, or alter the formatting of a piece of text, first 'select' the area of text that you wish to change.

- To delete a block of text, select it in the normal way and press the Delete key.

- Try clicking on a number of dropdown menus to acquaint yourself with their actions.

- Don't forget to save your work at regular intervals.

- Add new folders to the Documents library and put your files in them, so you can find the files more easily.

- Play around with this application to gain more confidence in the use of the keyboard, mouse and trackpad — you can always delete your efforts and start again if it all looks like a disaster zone.

Brain training

There may be more than one correct answer to the following questions.

1. How would you find the WordPad application?

a) On a tile on the Start screen

b) By typing 'wordpad' on the Start screen

c) By clicking on the Start button

d) By using the Search facility on the Charms menu

2. What is a cursor?

a) An alternative name for the mouse pointer

b) A flashing vertical line in the typing area of a word processor

c) An option found in the File menu

d) The point where any typing will be inserted

3. How would you save a document?

a) Choose Save from the File menu

b) It is not necessary — all documents are saved automatically

c) Use Ctrl+S

d) Click on the Save icon in the Quick Access bar

4. Which of the following statements is correct?

a) The Backspace key removes characters to the right of the cursor

b) The Delete key removes characters to the right of the cursor

c) The Delete key removes all the selected text

d) The Navigation keys remove text in the direction of the arrow

Answers

Q1 – a, b and d

Q3 – a, c and d

Q2 – b and d

Q4 – b and c

Getting help

Equipment needed: A computer (laptop, tablet or desktop), Windows 8 operating system, monitor screen, preferably with touchscreen capability, keyboard and mouse or trackpad and a printer.

Skills needed: Keyboard and mouse (Chapter 1), knowledge of the Desktop interface (Chapter 3) and familiarity with windows (Chapter 4).

Computers can be frustrating, stubborn and unpredictable at times but in spite of their faults they often try to help you solve problems that arise. Unlike car manuals, which are useless if the reversing lights stop working, computers are getting quite good at this sort of thing.

First of all, if the computer seems to have stopped reacting to your input from the keyboard or mouse, check to see whether it is waiting for you to do something before it can continue its work. You may see a flashing icon along the bottom of the screen. Click on this — it might be asking for your permission to complete a particular action such as saving a file, inserting a CD or topping up a low battery.

Help menus

Almost every computer application or app offers a Help facility. The icon for this (see Figure 9.1) is usually at the top-right end of the Menu bar. Click on the icon to access the Help menu.

Figure 9.1

Older programs load the Help files when the program is initially installed but recently developed apps and applications need an Internet connection to access the files on the web. This saves disk space on your machine and keeps the information up to date. The Internet is covered in Chapters 10 and 13.

A quicker way to raise the Help menu for a particular app or application is to use the F1 key towards the top left of the keyboard. Tapping this key immediately raises the relevant Help screen. This does not apply to all applications but is always worth a try.

Whatever method you use, you will be presented with a window that looks like Figure 9.2, which shows the initial Help page for WordPad. A few suggested help topics are listed on the right of the page but if you need assistance on a specific topic you will need to place the cursor in the Search box and type in a word or phrase relevant to your problem. There will be times when you find yourself stuck for an answer to an apparently simple question. For instance, you may want to do something you have never previously attempted, such as create a table within a document or insert a symbol such as the Euro sign. Simply type in the word 'table' or 'symbol', click on the magnifying glass to the right of the box and the instructions will appear in front of you — sometimes in the form of a tutorial.

If the instructions are lengthy it may be easier to print out the advice by clicking on the Print icon or using the keyboard shortcut of Ctrl+P.

Always try to use a Help function before asking your guardian angel for help. You will learn more quickly if you discover the answer for yourself rather than being shown by someone else.

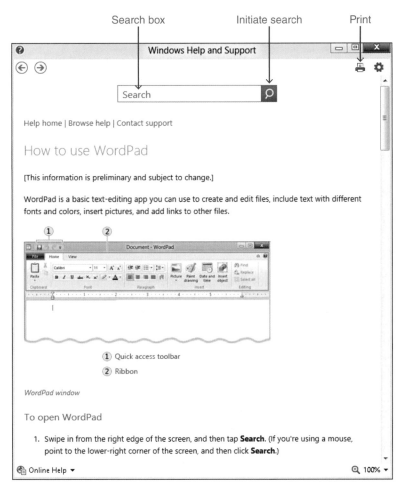

Figure 9.2

Windows Help facility

Not only does every program come with its own Help features but the Windows 8 operating system also offers a very extensive Help function, which will answer most of your questions about how your computer works. This can be a very useful teaching aid. For instance, you may want to know what the different shapes of pointer imply or how to create new folders and move files between different folders. Access this useful tool by typing the word 'help' when the Start screen is showing. Tap or click on the Help tile to open the Help application screen (see Figure 9.3).

Figure 9.3

In Figure 9.3, we have clicked on the Browse Help option and the screen is showing a small part of the broad range of assistance on offer. More specific questions can be asked by typing a suitable word or phrase in the Search box. The Windows Help files were installed on your computer when the system was first set up and are automatically kept up to date with new features and applications. In the bottom left of this window, there is a button that says Online Help. This implies you are connected to the Internet, so when you search for something you will be searching a wider database. If the button says Offline Help, you are not connected to the Internet but can still search the local help files.

Raise the Help screen in the way previously described, tap or click on the Browse icon and then choose Getting Started. You will find a lot of information that is very useful not only to beginners but also to more experienced users.

Getting help from the Internet

We have yet to explore the possibilities of the Internet, which we do in later chapters. It can be an invaluable source of assistance. Many is the time we have been completely baffled by a problem only to find the answer on the web. Services such as Google can quickly provide those elusive answers, and video tutorials on most aspects of computing can be found on the Internet. We will be discussing the uses of the Internet in Chapter 13.

Hung programs

Not a form of capital punishment for a criminal application, but a well-recognised computing term. There will be times when a program gets 'stuck' and refuses to respond to commands. Nothing you do makes any difference — no amount of clicking, tapping or typing has any effect at all. When a program acts like this it is said to have 'hung'. You may see the words Not Responding in the title bar. If you are lucky it may correct itself after a few minutes but if nothing has happened after five minutes, you will need to shut the program down using the Task Manager.

Task Manager

If you are using an application from the desktop and it hangs, you can raise the Task Manager by right-clicking on the taskbar at the bottom of the window. You can also use the key combination of Ctrl+Alt+Del all together, which raises a screen on which one of the options is the Task Manager.

If an app hangs, go to the Start screen, where there should be a Task Manager tile. If you are unable to find the tile, type the word 'task' onto the Start screen and the computer will find it for you.

The Windows 8 Task Manager (see Figure 9.4) is a much more comprehensive utility than previous Windows versions. It is now so comprehensive that you may find yourself very confused! In practice, beginners only need to pay attention to the Processes tab, which displays any applications that are currently running on the computer. The hung program will be identified by the words "not responding" after the program title. Tap or click on the offending app and then tap or click on the End Task button in the bottom-right corner.

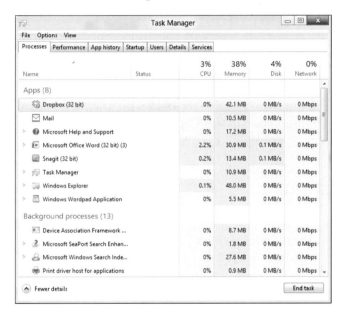

Figure 9.4

Feel free to explore the other tabs but please do not attempt to alter any of the settings at this stage. That is a job for your guardian angel.

After you have closed the errant program down you will almost certainly be able to reopen it without the problem.

Be aware that when you use the Task Manager to end a program, you may lose all or part of the work you completed before the program became hung. That's why, if a program does not respond to a command, it is always a good idea to wait for a few minutes to see if it will repair itself. Another good reason to save your work on a regular basis so that you can reload a recently saved version.

Keyboard shortcuts

Instead of tapping or clicking numerous icons and buttons, you can speed up your computing by using keyboard shortcuts. There are hundreds of these shortcuts — we have already mentioned a few. Some of them will prove very useful in your day-to-day work. These shortcuts are activated by holding down one or more of the modifying keys, such as Alt, Ctrl or Shift, while simultaneously pressing another key. Table 9.1 shows some of the most useful shortcuts.

Table 9.1: Helpful shortcuts

Keyboard shortcut	Action
Ctrl+C	Copies an item
Ctrl+X	Cuts and copies an item
Ctrl+V	Pastes a previously copied item
Ctrl+Z	Undoes a previous action
Ctrl+P	Prints
Ctrl+A	Selects a whole document
Ctrl+F	Finds a word in a document
F1	Raises the Help menu
Alt+F4	Closes the program
Esc	Cancels a current process
Ctrl+E	Centres the text on the page
Ctrl+L	Moves the cursor to the left edge of the page
Ctrl+R	Moves the cursor to the right edge of the page
Ctrl+B	Emboldens the selected text

There may be occasions when the computer simply fails to respond. In this case there is one final option you can try: shutting down the computer completely. In the Charms window, select Shutdown (not Restart) from the Settings menu. This will often kick the computer back into behaving properly. The problem may have been due to a corrupted file getting stuck somewhere in the system, which can only be rectified by closing the whole system down and starting afresh.

Last resort

If you try all the options and you cannot get either the app or the computer to respond, press the power on/off button and keep pressing it. After a few seconds the computer will turn off. Yes, this is a bit drastic but there are occasions when it will be the only option.

Summary

- Almost all programs provide a Help facility, although some are better than others.

- If in doubt, press the F1 key to raise the Help menu.

- Use the Windows 8 Help and Support option to expand your knowledge of the use of the computer.

- For more detailed help with computer problems, use the Internet.

- Use the Task Manager to close down non-responding programs.

- Access the Task Manager by right-clicking on an application taskbar or using the Start screen search facility.

- Keyboard shortcuts will often speed up your computing skills.

Brain training

There may be more than one correct answer to the following questions.

1. How can you get help if you are stuck?

a) Use the Internet

b) Press the F1 key

c) Click on the question mark icon

d) Ask your guardian angel

2. What action would Ctrl+P perform?

a) Pause a video

b) Print a document or photo

c) Display your latest photos

d) Access a phone on the computer

3. How would you access the Task Manager?

a) Press Alt+T

b) Tap or click on the Task Manager tile

c) Type 'task' into the Start screen

d) Right-click on the Desktop screen

4. What is a hung program?

a) A minimised application

b) A program stored in the temporary memory of the computer

c) A program that is no longer supported by the manufacturer

d) A program or app that has stopped working for some reason

Answers

Q1 — All four answers are correct but answer d should be used as a last resort

Q2 — b

Q3 — b, c and d

Q4 — d

PART III
Connecting and Protecting

That's the secret password, firewall and encryption sorted, now I'd like a Martini —shaken, not stirred.

Connecting to the Internet

Equipment needed: None.

Skills needed: An interest in knowing how your computer connects with the outside world.

So far, most of what we have done has used nothing more than the stand-alone computer. But there is another universe out there called the Internet, or the World Wide Web, and this huge resource is just waiting for you at the end of a telephone line. Windows 8 makes greater use of the Internet than any previous operating system.

How the Internet works

Unfortunately, accessing the Internet is not simply a matter of plugging the computer into the telephone socket and typing — you need a system to connect your home computer to the Internet. This is where Internet Service Providers (ISPs) come in. These companies have computer 'servers' that receive your requests and messages and transmit them, via a global network of wires, satellites and cables, to other servers that either contain the information you have requested or store your email messages until the recipient is ready to receive them. The Internet is simply a lot of networks talking to each other. It is not 'owned' by any individual or organisation, although it is regulated by a number of international organisations.

Many people refer to the Internet and World Wide Web (or just 'the web') as the same thing. This is not exactly accurate. The Internet is the network of connections between computers; the Web is the information held by those computers.

Figure 10.1 shows how home computers are linked to each other by means of ISP servers and the Internet. Let us assume that Alice, sitting at computer A wishes to send a message to Brad at computer B, by email. She also wants to send a copy of the email to Carol at computer C. She types Brad and Alice's email addresses into the address box, types out the message on her computer and 'sends' it via the telephone network or cable connection. The email is then received by her ISP mail server. Mail servers act in much the same way as postal sorting offices, and are in communication with other mail servers around the globe.

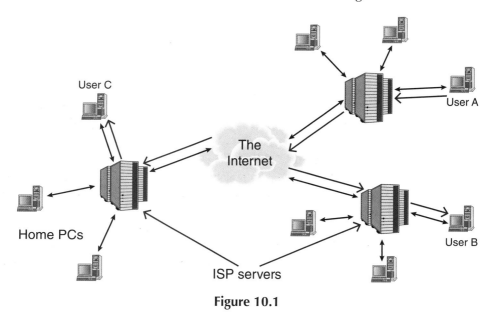

Figure 10.1

Alice's ISP mail server analyses the addresses and sends one copy to Brad's ISP and another to Carol's ISP. The messages are then held in Brad and Carol's personal mailboxes until their ISP servers receive instructions to download the messages onto Brad and Carol's respective home computers. If you have a broadband connection via telephone or cable, your personal computer will usually (not all mail programs automatically download messages) check the mailboxes on a regular basis to see if there are any messages waiting to be downloaded. It is rather like the postman delivering the mail but, unlike the postal service, there are many deliveries every day and it's much faster than 'snailmail'. If you are 'online' (connected to the Internet), you will receive an email within a few minutes of someone sending it to you.

The Internet doesn't just send email messages — you can also use it to get information from the Web or book an airline ticket. For example, if Carol wants to shop online, she simply connects to the retailer's website via the Internet and types in her order. In this case, instead of communicating with individuals at their personal computers, she links up with the large computers that service the retail stores' websites. We will be exploring the mechanics of information gathering and online shopping in later chapters.

Internet Service Providers (ISPs)

As we mentioned earlier, you need the services of an Internet Service Provider (ISP) to access the Internet. How do you get one? You won't have seen an ISP shop on the high street but you won't have seen an electricity shop either and that doesn't stop you from getting electricity. You will find ISPs listed in the Yellow Pages but we would not recommend this approach for beginners, as ISPs listed in directories tend to be local specialist providers that offer an Internet service alongside their computer repair and sales services. You will be better served by one of the national or international ISPs. Here we find ourselves in a Catch 22 situation. The normal method of contacting an ISP provider is via the Internet but, until you have subscribed to an ISP, you cannot access the Internet. This is where your guardian angel can help. He or she will have no difficulty setting up your connection whereas it could prove to be a minefield for the beginner. (This is explained later in the chapter.)

There are many ISPs vying for your custom in the marketplace, such as BT, Virgin, TalkTalk and even the Post Office, to name but a few. You may have seen adverts for some of them, on TV or on hoardings. Flick through the pages of any computer magazine and you will find a glut of advertisements offering 'the best service you can buy'. This exercise not only leaves you spoilt for choice but, more importantly, totally confused. You do not have the knowledge yet to understand most of the content of the magazines, nevermind evaluate the conflicting claims of the various ISP companies. Faced with this wealth of alternatives, how do you make a choice with so little knowledge? And that's before you address the question of how much it is likely to cost — access to the Internet does not come free and you will have to take out a monthly subscription with your chosen ISP. The cost can vary widely. This is where your guardian angel comes in handy.

Choosing an ISP

When choosing a car we often seek advice from friends and family. We don't have to take their advice but it forms part of our decision-making process. You can do the same thing when you choose an ISP. You could ask a neighbour about the kind of service they get from their ISP company. By choosing the same company, you will be able to discuss problems (should you experience any) over a friendly cup of tea. This is also something you should definitely discuss with your guardian angel or even the outlet that sold you the computer in the first place. You could reasonably ask one or the other to set you up with a reputable ISP. Unless you are brimming with confidence, which is unlikely at this stage of your computing career, we would not suggest that you try doing this yourself.

Part of your decision will depend upon the connections you may have in your house. If you have only a fixed telephone line, you may have fewer choices than if you have a cable TV connection.

Before you can make a telephone connection to an ISP, the telephone company will have to make a few minor alterations to your telephone connection at the exchange and you will need to plug a small filter into all your phone sockets throughout the house. These filters will be sent to you by the ISP together with an installation disk and, possibly, a router. A router is a small box that you connect to your telephone socket. It receives Internet signals, which it then broadcasts to your computer. The router will usually have a wireless facility, which allows you to connect your computer to the Internet wirelessly, by means of a radio connection to the router. This is known as a Wi-Fi connection. You should only need one router, no matter how many computers you have in the house. If your router is connected to the computer by wires, it's best to have them close to each other to avoid the risk of tripping over loose cables running across the floor. Long cables may also degrade the quality of the Internet reception.

Do not use extension cables between the telephone socket and the router. The broadband Internet signals do not travel well across extension plugs.

Broadband

You may have heard the word 'broadband' used by computer aficionados and not had a clue what on earth they are talking about. No, it is not a wide elastic band. It's useful to imagine broadband as a road carrying traffic. When a village served by the road grows into a small town, the original road network will become congested with traffic and wider roads will be needed.

Broadband is the road along which the Internet signals travel: in other words, it is what allows you to use your telephone connection to access the Internet as well as the phone. The broader the 'band', the more traffic it can handle. More and more people are joining the Internet every week, putting more and more strain on the existing network and slowing the traffic to a crawl, so the ISP companies have to keep increasing the capacity of their cable networks to accommodate them. Putting in broadband is the equivalent of putting in a dual carriageway. This is one of the reasons why Internet speeds can vary from one ISP to another. They only increase the capacity when the demand slows up the connection.

Internet videos require a good broadband speed. Even if you are not interested in the latest pop videos, you can access countless other videos online and you are bound to find something to appeal to you. Video tutorials and repeats of TV programmes will increase your use and enjoyment of the home computer so opt for a reasonably fast Internet connection.

Only a few years ago, broadband service was rarely available outside larger towns and rural populations had to make do with a much slower connection service called 'dialup'. Figures vary, but it is believed that more than 90% of the UK population now has access to broadband if they want it, leaving only very remote areas reliant on the older method of connecting. The speed of communication is measured in megabits per second. This will mean very little to you so let us use an analogy: the dialup service ran at about the equivalent of 5 mph, whereas an average broadband connection conveys information at 300 – 400 mph, with some connections going even faster. The telephone system's old copper cabling can only maintain these speeds within three or four miles of the telephone exchange, after which they fall to about 40 mph. Newer fibre optic cabling, which is gradually being installed across the country, can achieve speeds equivalent to 2,000 mph. Speeds of 40 – 100 mph are more than adequate to cope with simple tasks, such as emailing and online shopping, but if you want to watch videos online, you will soon become frustrated by the frequent interruptions as the signals try to catch up with each other. Most ISPs can do a line test and advise you of the connection speed you are likely to get. You do not need to buy the service from that ISP but you can use the information when comparing providers.

Do not be swayed by ISP advertisements that suggest they offer speeds of up to 40 megabits (400 mph). The words 'up to' are all-important. Your distance from the telephone exchange is far more important to speed than anything the ISPs can do to increase that speed. We would always choose a company that offers a reasonable speed and good customer backup, rather than one that offers lightning speed communications but can never be contacted when things go wrong.

Internet costs

You can opt for a simple broadband connection, which will cost between £12 and £18 a month and provide good broadband speeds and an adequate download limit. If, like most people, you have a telephone account you will find that you can reduce the cost considerably, not only of your Internet connection but also of your telephone calls by combining various services. These types of contract are referred to as 'bundles'. With some companies, you can include the cost of your satellite TV viewing as well, while others will 'bundle' your mobile phone account in the package. Ask your guardian angel to investigate a price comparison site, such as Uswitch to check out the best value for money.

Be careful with your choice because these 'bundles' will tie you in to a contract for 12 to 18 months and there are hefty penalties for early termination of a contract.

We mentioned the term 'download limit' in the previous paragraph and this may have left you confused. Some ISP companies impose a limit on the amount of information you can access, or 'download', in any calendar month. Emails, information and online shopping are very economical and shouldn't eat into your limit too much, but if you are going to be downloading TV programmes, computer apps and applications, films and necessary updates to your existing programs, you may find that you exceed your allocated limit, thereby incurring extra charges. As a ballpark figure, you should allow for a download limit of 40 gigabytes per month or more. Downloading more than your limit will incur heavy charges so be careful so as to avoid a nasty surprise when your bill arrives.

To clarify a technical issue about bits and bytes: All computers work with ones and zeros, these are called bits. Computers use bits to transfer information but these are grouped together into larger units. Eight bits makes a byte. There are roughly 1,000 bytes in a kilobyte (KB); 1,000 kilobytes is a megabyte (MB) and 1,000 megabytes make a gigabyte (GB). Most computer disks can hold upwards of 500 gigabytes. This is more than enough for most computer users.

Setting up your Internet connection

Whoever is setting up your connection for you — probably your guardian angel — will need certain information from you in order to complete the registration process. At some point during the set up you will need to choose a username and password, which you will use when you communicate with the ISP.

Usernames

Your username is the name that identifies you to the ISP company, and this is always confirmed by a password. Your username may also be included as part of your email address that the ISP will allocate to you as part of the package.

You must choose a username that is unique. It's probably fine to use your given name if it happens to be Mathilde Onejaro, for example, but if your name is John Green the username 'johngreen' will certainly have been taken by someone else and you will have to give some thought to what you want your username to be. Perhaps you can incorporate your middle name or initial to come up with a solution like 'johnbgreen'. You do not have to use your name. If your name is William Thompson and you have a cat called Puffball, you could suggest 'thompuff' or 'puffthom' and get away with it. Usernames must not include a space but you can use symbols such as underscores or full stops. You'll notice we have used lower-case letters in our examples, and we suggest you do the same for your username. It is easier to remember it that way.

After you have chosen and entered a username, the ISP company will check that it is not being used by anyone else. If it is, it might suggest a viable alternative; for instance, you might be told that 'jacksonpollock' has been taken but 'jackson_pollock27' is available. Keep trying until you find a name that is unique to the ISP as well as acceptable and easily remembered by you.

When you're choosing your username, bear in mind that it may become part of your email address, which you will be giving to anyone you want to exchange emails with. So, for example, if you settle on a username of puffthom and you choose BT as your ISP, your email address will be **puffthom@btinternet.com**. All email addresses include the '@' character. We will cover emailing in Chapter 12.

Passwords

Passwords are used to confirm your identity. They should be a single block of eight or more characters, preferably longer. They should not be easily guessed by outsiders who may wish to gain access to your account for nefarious purposes. Your mother's maiden name or the name of your pet may be easily remembered but they can guessed by family and friends — not to mention the rogues of the computing world. Your password does not have to make sense. You can use upper and lower case characters, symbols and numbers to create strong passwords. The top five most common passwords used on the Internet are '1234', '123456', '12345678', 'password' and 'iloveyou' — all of which can be guessed by criminal minds trying to access your account. Think laterally. Perhaps your favourite book as a child was Five Go to Treasure Island so you could adapt this as a password such as '5gotoTrls'. Very few people will guess this combination. If your ISP allows you to have a longer password, try the phrase treasureisland itself. You might want to make it even more difficult to guess by using different cases and numbers, as in tRea5ure1slaNd. The longer a password is, the more secure it is.

Payment

You will have to provide your ISP with your credit card or bank account details to allow payment of your monthly bill by direct debit. It is very understandable that computing beginners feel rather uncertain about releasing these financial details over the Internet. The question of financial security is covered in Chapter 11.

After the necessary details have been entered and your contract accepted, you will be welcomed by your new ISP. A frisson of nervous excitement may run down your spine as you dash off your first email to your nephew in Australia. Well, not quite. You may have to wait for about 30 minutes while the ISP sets up your account on its own network to receive instructions from your home computer. Welcome to the world of the Internet and the World Wide Web.

Summary

- You will need the services of an Internet Service Provider (ISP) to access information on the Internet and send emails.

- Broadband is a fast communication system enabling your computer to access the Internet.

- You can considerably reduce your monthly charges by opting for a 'bundled' package.

- Choose a password that is difficult for other people to guess but easy for you to memorise.

- Wireless communication reduces the need for physical wiring, which may constitute a tripping hazard.

- Do not use extension cables to connect the router to the telephone socket.

- Do not expect your connection to achieve the speeds advertised by ISP companies.

- The Internet is a network of communications, while the web is the information held at the end of that network.

- Choose an ISP with a minimum download limit of 40 gigabytes or more.

Brain training

There may be more than one correct answer to the following questions.

1. What is an ISP?

   a)   An Independent Service Program

   b)   An Initial Stage Protocol

   c)   A service only used by large commercial organisations

   d)   An Internet Service Provider

2. What is broadband?

   a)   A digital TV connection

   b)   A fast connection to the Internet

   c)   An email program

   d)   A very large undersea cable linking continents

3. What is the Internet?

   a)   A network of communications spread across the globe

   b)   An international body that polices computer traffic

   c)   The internal wiring of a computer

   d)   A telephone network connecting different offices of the same company

4. Which of the following are suitable passwords?

   a)   Password

   b)   Your surname

   c)   rU$$ian5

   d)   Gl3nC0E

Answers

Q1 – d

Q3 – a

Q2 – b

Q4 – c and d

Protecting yourself online

Equipment needed: A computer (laptop, tablet or desktop), Windows 8 operating system, monitor screen, preferably with touchscreen capability, keyboard and mouse or trackpad. An Internet connection.

Skills needed: Keyboard and mouse (Chapter 1), knowledge of the Desktop interface (Chapter 3) and familiarity with windows (Chapter 4).

What is security?

You will be using your computer for a whole variety of purposes, including storing important personal records, photographs and music. You will also be using the Internet, where you may sometimes be asked to divulge personal details and credit card information. The big question is whether it is safe to store data on your computer permanently and to give out information on the Internet.

The answer is yes — providing you take the necessary precautions. This chapter looks at the risks and the precautions you can take to make yourself as safe as possible.

Security is all about common sense. Think about how you protect your property when you are out. You lock the doors and maybe have a burglar alarm. When you are shopping, you keep an eye on your purse or wallet, and shield your PIN number when you type it into a machine. We are going to look at how you apply the same sort of precautions to the computer and the way you use it.

Why do we need security? Unfortunately, we live in a world where some people are constantly looking for information about people like you. Their aim is identity theft, or to use the information for fraudulent purposes. Your personal information is valuable. It can be sold, then sold again, and before you know it, other people are using your identity.

The world of security consists of a myriad of strange terms that you may have seen bandied about. This section is designed to demystify some of those terms and give you a better understanding of this complex area.

Malware

Malware is the term used to describe any malicious software. This includes viruses, Trojans, hoaxes and others. Malware is a big problem because there are now so many methods that can be used to disrupt your computer or gather information from you. Some programs are there simply to annoy people but others may try to sell you software you don't need or take information from your computer.

Viruses

We hear a lot about computer viruses but what are they? Well, they act in much the same way as viruses that make you ill. There are many thousands of computer viruses and if your computer picks up one of them, it may act in a strange way. Perhaps files will start to disappear or the computer won't start.

How do viruses get onto computers? The most common way is when people open a file attached to an email they have been sent, and the file is not what it seems. The scoundrels who launch these things normally prey on human nature so you may open your mailbox to find an email titled something like 'Congratulations on your lottery win, click here to claim your reward'. You click on the file and the virus gets installed on your machine without you knowing about it. Your computer can also pick up a virus if you download music and videos from some of the illegal downloading sites. The people that run such sites have no scruples — they want your money or personal details, and might give you a virus as a reward.

After the virus has installed itself on your computer it may not show itself immediately. Some viruses only act on certain dates, such as anniversaries of major events, but will quietly spread on your machine, infecting files other than the one it arrived with. The virus won't spread to other computers unless you physically send or copy the file onto another computer — but of course you are unlikely to know the virus is there in the first place.

What can we do about viruses?

The two main actions you can take are to protect your computer and take care of what you do with your computer.

We protect computers with what is known as antivirus software. After this software is installed, your files will be protected and the software will monitor everything you do, checking to see if there is a virus present. If it detects a virus, a message will pop up on the screen informing you of what it has found and what it has done about it. Some viruses can just be cleaned but others get put into 'quarantine'. This is a safe area of the disk that is not used and keeps the file out of harm's way.

There is a good chance that when you buy a new computer it will already have some antivirus software installed. This may be a trial version, however, in which case you will have to pay to have it permanently installed. You may be lucky and get a year's subscription with your new computer.

If your computer does not arrive with antivirus software it's important to get some as soon as possible because as soon as you connect to the Internet your computer is at risk. There are many suppliers of antivirus software, including Norton, AVG and Kaspersky, to name a few. The prices are all much the same and there is no one product that is much better than another. Speak to other people about which product they have chosen.

When you install the software you will have to go to the Internet to get the latest virus information for the software. This needs to be done on a regular basis but your software should do it automatically. If your computer asks if you want it to update the antivirus software, you should always answer yes. That way, you will stay protected against any new viruses that appear.

Antivirus software will also protect you against Trojans and some forms of other malicious software.

Trojans

Think of the Trojan horse that was used to sneak the Greeks into the city of Troy. The Trojans were deceived because they thought the horse was a gift. The name has now been given to any software that arrives on your computer without your knowledge or permission. A Trojan will usually arrive as an attachment to an email message. It may look harmless, perhaps like an image or a game for you to try. You click on the attachment, thinking it is harmless, and the damage is done. What will it do? That depends upon the Trojan. It may collect a record of every key you press so it can capture passwords and credit card numbers; or it may allow your computer to be used remotely by hackers. You may be getting worried but you should be okay provided you have up-to-date antivirus software, which will detect Trojans as well as viruses and prevent them from running on your computer.

Hoaxes

When is a virus not a virus? When it is a hoax. Let's say you receive an email with the title, 'Warning: a new virus has been discovered – tell your friends'. This email may have come from a friend, as the message will usually advise recipients to pass the message on.

The email tells you of a terrible new virus that will delete all the files on your computer if you don't take the appropriate action. It may then ask you to do something to your computer, such as search for particular files and delete them. In some cases it might not matter if you delete the files but in others they might be important files the computer needs.

This message is a hoax. There is no new virus, and the email's purpose is purely to trick you into doing something then spread it to other people. What should you do? Delete it. Do not send it to your friends and family. If there is a new virus, your antivirus software will deal with it for you. If you are in any doubt, enter some key words from the message, followed by the word 'hoax' into the Google search box. The results will alert you to whether it is a recognised hoax.

Financial transactions

The Internet is enormously useful for buying things online. When you do this, you will be required to enter your personal details along with credit card details to complete the transaction. This can be a worrying process for beginners. What is happening to those details? Where are they going? There are risks attached to providing information like this but, with care, Internet shopping is as safe as shopping in the high street. We will now look at the various security issues that may arise with regard to personal information.

Phishing

Once you are connected to the Internet and are using email, you may start receiving emails from banks — both your own bank and banks you do not have an account with. The emails might tell you that your account has been suspended, or that you need to provide personal information. You will probably receive emails telling you that you have won lotteries that you haven't entered or that there are parcels waiting to be delivered to you. These messages are phishing emails, and they're nothing to do with catching carp. They are sent out in their thousands, in the hope that someone will read the email and follow the instructions, which usually asks you to click on a link that leads to a form that asks you to fill in the details of your bank account and, more importantly, security information like your password.

You will soon get used to spotting these because the wording of these messages is usually very poor, with incorrect spelling and grammar, and they often start 'Dear valued customer'. An example of a phishing email is shown in Figure 11.1. They tend not to be of the quality you would expect from a bank! This is where the delete key comes in handy again. Delete the email and do not follow the instructions.

Subject: Security Check From Chase
From: Chase@emailinfo.chase.com
Date: Mon, 17 Jan 2011 16:43:56 -0500

Dear Valued JPMorgan Chase Customer,

Due to a recent security check on JPMorgan Chase online banking on 15th
We require you to confirm your details and Re-activate your account

Re-activate now

Failure to do this within 24hrs will lead to access suspension
Sorry for the inconvienence

Regards
JPMorgan Chase Online Banking
Issued for USA use only | JPMorgan Chase Bank plc 2011

Figure 11.1

The purpose of these emails is to get you to part with private information such as the username and password you use for your banking. Your bank will *never* ask you to verify details over the Internet. Once you get used to the format of phishing emails you'll find they're easily recognised. If you receive a message from your bank that you are not sure of, don't do anything on the computer but telephone the bank and ask them to verify the message.

Encryption

Encryption is a process where confidential information you send on the Internet is encoded. This is particularly useful when you are purchasing something and are providing your personal details. When you use the Web, all the information flowing between you and the website is normally visible. Don't worry about this because at this stage you have nothing to hide. When you want to pay for an item, however, you don't want your personal information to be seen by other people, so the connection is automatically encrypted.

Let us say you are purchasing an item from an online retailer called website.com. You select the item and place it in the shopping basket, then select the Checkout option. At this point, if you look closely you will see a few changes on the web page. Where the address line at the top usually says http://www.website.com it will now say https://www.website.com. The 's' stands for 'secure'. You will also see a padlock on the address line. If you hover the cursor over the padlock it should actually display the name of the website you are connected to.

Figure 11.2 shows the 'https' in the address field and the information box that appears when you hover over the padlock. Note that the names match. This means that the connection between you and the web server, and all the information flowing between the two of you, is now encrypted thus making it secure for you to enter your credit card details safely. You don't have to do anything — this is an automatic process.

Source: www.amazon.co.uk

Figure 11.2

Encryption is also used for your wireless connection at home. More of this topic later.

Use of credit cards

Credit card details can safely be entered providing you have a secure connection. If you do not see the 'https' prefix in the address line, do not enter your details because your card number could be visible to others.

If you are happy that the connection is secure and you enter your details, you may then be asked by the website if you would like it to store your card details for it to use if you shop with the site again. This is purely a matter of personal choice. If you decline, you will just need to enter your details again the next time you buy from the site; if you agree, the site will ask you if it should use the card details it has on file. This can simplify the process, and means you don't have to enter the details every time you buy from the site. My details are stored with the website Amazon and this has never caused a problem.

Regular purchasing habits

After you have a purchase history with an online supplier, they will often send you emails with special offers or inform you, for example, of a sequel to a book you have bought has been published. This can be useful or it can be a nuisance. Usually a site will have a box you can tick to elect not to receive such communications. When you are a user of an online supplier, you will have to set up an account with a username, which will typically be your email address, and a password.

 Don't use the same password for all your online accounts. You don't need to set a different password for every account because that becomes difficult to manage but you could use a few different passwords spread across the accounts. That way, if someone discovers one of your passwords they won't have access to all of your accounts.

It is important to ensure that your antivirus protection is up to date because some of the malicious software looks for purchasing habits so it can build a profile of your Internet usage then target you with unwanted emails and pop-up adverts. Someone might also try and trick you into shopping from a rogue website by offering you goods similar to the ones you are known to have purchased. Once again, you do not need to worry if you have taken the necessary precautions.

Personal records

You will end up storing a lot of personal information on your computer. It is important that that only you, or those you trust, have access to your computer. This can be done by setting good passwords on the computer (see Chapter 2).

Backing up

Once you have been using your computer for a while, you will have all sorts of personal files stored on it. In addition to personal documents, you probably have photographs from your digital camera stored on the computer's hard disk, as well as your music collection.

All these files are stored safely on the computer disk but what happens if the disk suddenly becomes faulty? Modern technology is very reliable but these things can still go wrong. If the hard disk in the computer develops a fault, that special wedding video and those vital documents might be lost forever.

This is where you need to think about taking precautions by making a duplicate, or backup, of your files for safety purposes.

External backup

The easiest way of protecting these files is to make a copy of them onto another disk. You may decide to purchase another hard disk drive on which to store your backup files. You can purchase an external drive from a large supermarket or electrical retailer, or online from a company like Amazon. There is a range of sizes available but the size you choose will depend on how much data you want to back up. A 500-gigabyte drive will cost about £40.

Plug the cable from the drive into one of your computer's sockets (called USB sockets) and open the Desktop screen. You will see that the new device has appeared on the screen and has used another letter (like D). To make a backup copy of your files, left-click on the files you wish to save and drag them onto the new drive letter. They will then be copied onto the external drive. Once the process is complete, disconnect the drive by unplugging it and store the drive in a safe place. Do not store the drive near the computer because if something happens to the computer (such as a fire or theft) you will lose both. You could even let a friend look after the drive. It is always better to be safe. Get into the habit of backing up regularly, especially when you have saved something important.

If you only have a small amount of data to back up, rather than buying a hard drive you could purchase a USB stick drive. This has a much smaller capacity (typically a few gigabytes) but is also cheaper. USB sticks are usually available in supermarket electrical sections and can cost as little as £5.

When you plug in an external storage device, Windows 8 helps by asking if you want to back up certain files. Figure 11.3 shows the screen that appears when you insert a device and select the option Configure this Drive for Backup. The computer will then automatically copy your most important files to the device. This will include documents, photos, videos and music. It's easy — every time you plug the device in it will save the latest copies.

Figure 11.3

Cloud

This is the latest buzzword that is floating around. Clouds allow you to store your data somewhere on the Internet, rather than on a device kept by you. Once you have arranged access with the cloud provider, you can store all the data you like in that provider's cloud. It is called the cloud because you don't know exactly where your data is but you can see it and access it. The cloud provider will make sure your data is always available and that there are copies in case of failure, so you don't have to worry about a thing. The advantage is that your files are safe and accessible, providing you can get to the Internet; the downside is that you have to pay for the service.

Microsoft's cloud is called Skydrive. It gives you some free storage in the cloud and you can then opt to pay for more. Google offers a large amount of storage for about £3.50 per month and a company called Livedrive offers a similar service for around £4 per month. Look into what they offer and work out what suits you.

Is it safe to use one of these services? Yes, because these are reputable companies that depend upon good service for their reputation.

Dropbox

One other program we would like to talk about is Dropbox, which is a way of storing your files in a cloud while also allowing other people to access those files. You get a certain amount of storage free and when you introduce friends you get more free space. The beauty of this is that not only can you save files by putting them in Dropbox but you can also create areas to share with your friends, so for example, you could put some holiday photos into a folder in Dropbox, give permission for your friends to access that folder and they can see the photos but not your private files. This is great for groups that want to share information about such things as hobbies. Dropbox can be found at **www.dropbox.com**.

Wi-Fi security

In Chapter 10, we stated that you may have a wireless connection to the Internet. To set this up, you will probably need the help of your guardian angel because part of the setup process requires you to set up encryption. This provides a secure connection for your computer to connect to the broadband router. For the technically minded, wireless security has strange titles, such as WEP, WPA or WPA2.

You (or more probably, your guardian angel) should always go for the strongest security possible, which is called WPA2. This requires a password that can be quite long so instead of thinking of a single word, think of a phrase that is easy to remember. For example, the phrase 'I love the sun shining' is simple but it makes a long, very strong password. Provided you keep it secret, you will have a very secure system that is difficult to break into. The ISP that has provided your wireless router may have already set up the password. In that case, all you have to do is type it into any computer where you want to use the wireless connection. When your computer has connected to a wireless network one time, it will remember it, so you should not have to keep entering the security parameters. Figure 11.4 shows you what you see when you open up the Settings option in the Charms menu. The icon in the top left indicates that wireless networks are available.

Figure 11.4

Many places now offer wireless networks for you to use when you are out and about with your laptop: hotels, coffee shops and restaurants, and your friends may have wireless networks too. If you are going to use one of these networks, think of security. Is it a secure network with encryption? If you have to ask the coffee shop or hotel for a password to access it, it should be secure. If you can connect to it without a password it is insecure. This means it is fine to use it to browse websites but it would be unwise to type in any personal information or credit card information. This is because it's possible that other users in the same area could connect to your computer.

The same rules always apply: you should be safe if you think about what you are doing. Figure 11.5 shows the networks that are visible if you click the Available button shown in Figure 11.4. There are exclamation marks by two of the networks (dlink and Sgn), indicating that they are insecure, with no encryption. If you hover the mouse pointer over the exclamation mark, a message appears stating that the network is insecure.

Figure 11.5

Firewalls

One last term to deal with is the firewall. A firewall is a device that acts as a barrier between you and the outside world. A firewall will prevent unwanted or unauthorised access to your computer from the Internet or other computers. A firewall can be a piece of software or a physical device. In our case, we don't need to worry because Windows comes with a built-in firewall which is configured to run automatically. You may also have an additional firewall as part of your broadband router. This is not a problem, in fact it gives you two layers of protection. It is very unlikely that you will need to do anything with the Windows firewall but if you do, it can be found inside the Control Panel Security settings.

- Security is not just about worrying about entering a credit card number on to a web page. It involves asking questions such as: Is my computer secure, with a good password? Is my data safe from intruders?

- Do I have a copy of my data in case the disk drive in my computer fails?

- If I have a wireless connection at home, is it protected with a good level of security?

- Computer security is a bit like driving a car — you have to be aware of what is going on otherwise you could have an accident.

- It's important to have antivirus software on your computer. This will protect you against viruses, Trojans and some other malicious software.

- When supplying personal information online, providing you are careful with what you do and who you give your information to, the Internet can be a safe place.

Brain training

There may be more than one answer to the following questions.

1. Which is a problem — a virus or a hoax?

a) A virus

b) A hoax

c) Neither of them presents a problem

d) They are both problems

2. Which of the following might be a phishing email?

a) An email telling you you have won the EuroMillions lottery

b) An email about an angling competition

c) An email about a relative you didn't know you had, suddenly dying in Africa leaving you some money

d) An email from your building society asking you to validate your password

3. Which of the following are ways to back up your data?

a) An external disk drive

b) An external memory stick

c) Using a cloud

d) Saving files in Dropbox

4. What is the purpose of the padlock when browsing the Internet?

a) It protects your computer from theft

b) It shows that you are connected to the correct website

c) It proves that the connection to the website is encrypted

d) It stops your mouse from moving the cursor

5. Why is security so important when using a computer?

a) To ensure all your personal details are safe from theft

b) To prevent viruses from damaging your files

c) To stop you from browsing the Internet

d) To prevent your friends from sending you emails

Answers

Q1 – d

Q4 – b and c

Q2 – a, c and d

Q5 – a and b

Q3 – a, b, c and d

Using email

12

Equipment needed: A computer (laptop, tablet or desktop), Windows 8 operating system, monitor screen, preferably with touchscreen capability, keyboard and mouse or trackpad. You will also need an ISP Internet connection. A printer will be useful.

Skills needed: Keyboard and mouse (Chapter 1), knowledge of the Desktop interface (Chapter 3), familiarity with windows (Chapter 4), some experience with word processing (Chapter 8) and some idea of the Internet concept (Chapter 10).

The concept of email

Email allows you to send messages to Toronto, Teddington or Tajikistan in a matter of seconds and is the most common reason for people wanting to use a home computer. It's a very straightforward process — but that's easy for us to say, isn't it? You might feel clumsy and inept at first but, like learning to ride a bicycle, after a little practice, you will soon be sending and receiving messages with confidence.

Email is probably more reliable than letter post but this does rely upon a number of factors. First, as with ordinary letters, you must get the address exactly right. However, whereas if you address a letter incorrectly you won't know if it doesn't reach its destination, if you address an email incorrectly, you will usually get an instant reply saying that the address was not recognised.

Certain characters (such as - ( )[ ] \ ; : , < >) are never allowed in an email address while others (such as ! # $ % * / ? | ^ { } ` ~) may be rejected by some email services. If you stick with common letters and numbers you will be fine. Also bear in mind that if the addressee does not check their email regularly your message may lie unread in their mailbox for a while.

We explained how email works in Chapter 10: to recap, once you have sent your message it goes to your Internet Service Provider's (ISP's) computer, which routes it to the recipient's ISP where it is stored until the recipient connects to their own email, when it is delivered to their inbox.

Windows 8 email

You can use either the Start screen or the Desktop interface to send and receive email messages in Windows 8. In either case, you will need to have an email account set up.

Types of email address

There are two ways of obtaining an email address. The first is through your ISP, which will provide you with an address when you sign up to their service. In this case, your ISP's name will be included in the address (for example, joebloggs123@ btInternet.com or banjo78@talktalk.co.uk).

The second way is to create one yourself on the Internet. For instance, Google mail will offer an email address such as hans.fassbender@gmail.com while a Windows Live Mail address could be wi77ow@live.co.uk.

If at any time in the future you decide to change your ISP, you will lose your ISP email address and have to inform all your correspondents of your change of address. Internet-based email addresses will remain the same even if you change your ISP.

Setting up an email account

We will explain how to download and install applications, or programs, from the Internet in Chapter 15 but since you probably want to start sending emails as soon as possible it would be a good idea to get your guardian angel to set up your email facility at this stage. He or she will need to install a mail application and we suggest a suite of programs called Windows Live Essentials; this offers a photo gallery, a word processor and a video editing application as well, but we are only interested in its email function at this early stage.

Both Start screen and Desktop interfaces use the same email addresses but display the information in different ways.

Mail

The Mail tile will almost certainly be at the left end of the Start menu tiles (see Figure 12.1). Activate it by tapping or clicking on the tile. When the initial screen appears, access your email account by right-clicking or flicking sharply upwards from the bottom edge of the screen to display the menu options at the bottom of the screen. Click on the Accounts button to reveal the accounts set up on your system. If you are using Windows Live Essentials, choose the Live Mail account. Those at Microsoft have changed the name of their live mail system several times now. The latest release is going to be called Outlook mail, however, the terms Hotmail and Live Mail are still in common use. All these systems work in the same way and use the same tile on the desktop. Having clicked on the account, you will probably see a rather blank page. Raise the menu bar again by right-clicking or flicking up from the bottom edge and click on Folders (see Figure 12.2).

Figure 12.1

Folders   Messages   Attachments   Selected message

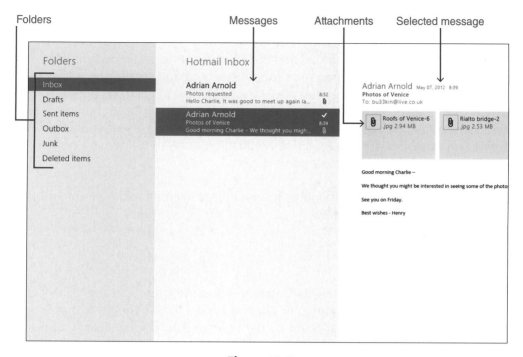

Figure 12.2

Folders

This screen normally opens with the contents of the Inbox displayed. View the contents of the other folders by clicking or tapping on their names.

Inbox

This folder contains the messages you have received. At this stage you will not have received any messages from friends or relatives but there may be one or two welcoming messages from Live Mail. Figure 12.2 shows the folders, a list of received messages and the contents of the selected message. By clicking on the Inbox folder you will remove the folder list, allowing more room for the list of messages and the message pane (see Figure 12.3).

New message   Send   Delete

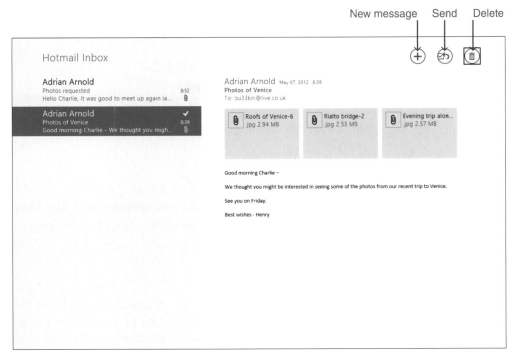

Figure 12.3

Drafts

This folder retains messages you have composed but not yet sent.

Sent items

As the name suggests, this folder holds copies of the messages you have sent to other people. If you are not sure whether a message has been sent, check in this folder.

Outbox

When you send a message it is posted to the Outbox, from which it is sent. This happens very quickly so this folder is likely to be empty most of the time. If you compose a message at a time when your computer is not connected to the

Internet, on a laptop, for example, the message will remain in the Outbox until the Internet connection is restored. It will then be sent automatically.

Junk

This folder contains messages that your email application believes to be junk mail, also known as 'spam'. We will talk about junk mail later in the chapter.

Deleted items

When you delete a message it is not lost forever but held in this folder. The messages only vanish completely when you delete the messages from this folder.

Sending an email

After you are set up, you can send your first message. Make sure you have the Inbox folder selected, which will look something like Figure 12.3. Click or tap on the New Message button in the top right to open up the message screen (see Figure 12.4).

Hopefully, your guardian angel or a few friends will have given you their email addresses but you can always send a message to yourself as practice. Click or tap in the To message box and type in the address of the person to whom you want to send your message. The Cc address box is for the addresses of anyone else to whom you want to send a copy of the email.

Email addresses never have a space in them and always contain the @ symbol. Make sure that you type in the address accurately.

Address boxes   Main message area   Subject line   Send button   Delete or Save

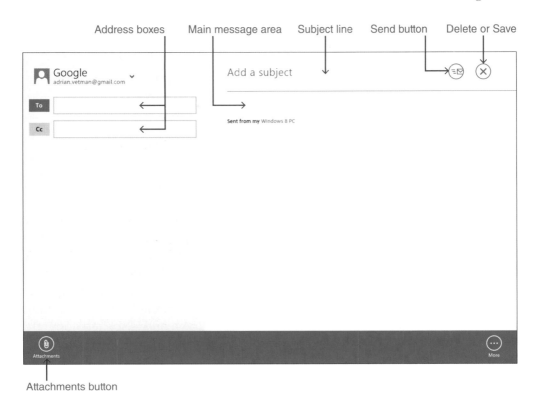

Attachments button

Figure 12.4

It is good practice to add a subject header to your messages to allow the recipient to identify individual messages. To add a subject header, tap or click on the words "Add a subject", which will disappear leaving a flashing cursor in their place, allowing you to type the subject header. To compose the body of the message, tap or click at the top of the message area and begin typing your message. We covered the subject of word processing in Chapter 8 so if you are having any problems with typing, refer back to that chapter.

Spelling corrections

Unlike WordPad, Live Mail has an automatic spellchecker. Take a look at the sentence in Figure 12.5.

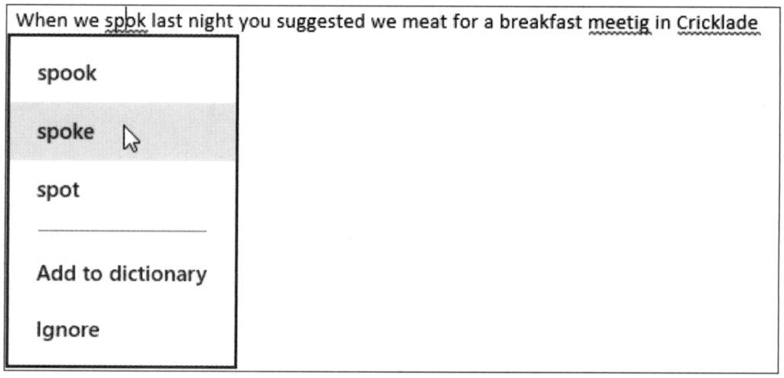

When we sppk last night you suggested we meat for a breakfast meetig in Cricklade

spook

spoke

spot

Add to dictionary

Ignore

Figure 12.5

There are two incorrectly spelled words, and Live Mail has automatically under-lined these in red. You could manipulate the cursor and correct them manually but there is a quicker way to do it. Right-click on one of the underlined words and a dropdown menu appears, offering alternative spellings. Left-click on the correct word and it will replace the incorrect spelling. In this example, there is a third underlined word, Cricklade, which is the name of a town and is spelled correctly. Right-click on the word and choose the Add to Dictionary option. The next time the word appears it will be accepted.

Do not rely on the spellchecker too heavily. Look at the sentence again and you will notice that the word "meat" should read "meet" but since both are recognised words the mistake has not been picked up by the spellchecker.

Once you have composed the message, send it by clicking or tapping on the Send button. The screen may show the word Syncing in the top-left corner of the screen, informing you that the message is being sent. Syncing is a term used quite regu-larly by Windows 8 and simply means that the computer is communicating with the Internet or another computer.

Congratulations! You have just sent your first email. You can make sure it has been sent by opening the Sent Items folder and checking a copy has been kept there.

Receiving an email

As long as your computer is turned on and connected to the Internet it will download any messages held by your ISP. The computer will check for new messages regularly but to check for very recent messages, click or tap on the Sync button on the left of the right-click menu at the bottom of the screen. Figures 12.2 and 12.3 show the layout of a received message. To display the contents of a particular email, click on the message you want to see from the list of messages.

Attachments

Emails are not restricted to text messages. You can also attach files to an email, such as minutes of a meeting, photos and financial reports. To attach a file to an email, raise the menu shown in Figure 12.6 by flicking or right-clicking on the message screen and selecting the Attachments button.

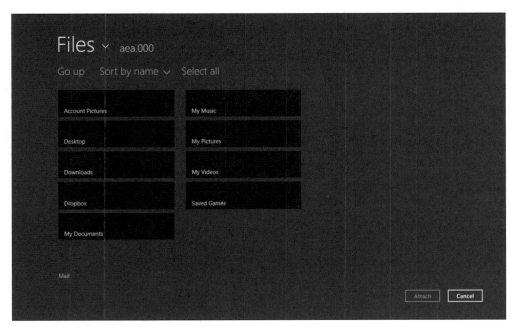

Figure 12.6

Navigate your way to the file you want to attach: select Documents if you want to send a document or My Pictures if you want to send a photo. As you navigate your way through the filing system you will eventually arrive at the folder containing the required file. Files available for attachment will appear in the right half of the screen. Click on the file and the Attach button in the bottom-right corner will light up. Click on this button to attach the file. You will be returned to the message screen where you will notice the file being loaded into the message. Wait for this to complete before sending the email or adding another file. You can usually attach at least 20 files to an email, depending on the size of the files.

Don't get too carried away with attachment files; some of them can be very large and take a long time to transmit and receive. For instance, an A4 letter may be 20 kilobytes and take half a second to transmit but a video may be anything up to 20 megabytes (a megabyte is 1,000 kilobytes) and take more than an hour unless you have a fast broadband connection. Videos and sound files are notoriously large, and some picture files can be large too.

Viewing attachments

When you receive an email, any attachments are shown across the top of the message (see the email in Figure 12.2, which has three photos attached to it). At this stage, the attachments are shown as square blocks. To open an attachment, click or tap on the filename and wait for it to download onto your computer. Depending on the size of the file and your Internet connection speed, this may take a couple of minutes. Even then it will only appear as a small thumbnail picture. To view the full size image, click on the thumbnail and the image will open in another application automatically. In your case, it will probably be the Live Gallery.

Spam or junk mail

Just as we all get far too much unsolicited junk mail in the post, the same problem arises with email. After you have been emailing for a few weeks your address will have found its way to marketing companies who will send you unsolicited messages promoting their wares. This junk mail is known in the computing world as 'spam'. Most email applications can identify such unwanted messages and consign them to the Junk folder. It is always worth checking the Junk folder periodically because the system is not perfect and the mail server may have categorised a message you were expecting as junk. If this is the case, simply drag the mail from the junk folder into the Inbox.

Never reply to spam messages. It only confirms to the sender that your email address is active and it will be passed around to other spammers, increasing the likelihood of even more unwanted mail. Spam may also contain viruses and other 'nasties' so try not to open them in case they infect your computer.

Replying and forwarding

To reply to a message, make sure the message is open and click or tap on the Respond button (see Figure 12.7). A new message screen will appear with the sender's email address already inserted in the address box. Compose your reply in the same way as you create an original message and click on the Send button. You can also Forward the message to other people, or choose Reply All to reply to everyone the original message was addressed to.

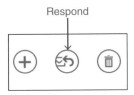

Figure 12.7

Deleting messages

Delete messages by using the Delete button, which looks like a dustbin (see Figure 12.7). The message will then automatically move from the Inbox folder to the Deleted folder.

Contacts

As you continue to use Windows 8 you will discover a faster way of entering email addresses using the People app on the Start screen. We will be covering this and other apps that interact with each other in Chapter 14.

Desktop mail

Using the Start screen Mail tile is the easiest way of accessing an email system on the desktop but there are other ways and other options for using email. You could, for example, just use Google mail from your web browser. Microsoft has a product called Live Mail, and some of you may have come across an earlier incarnation called Hotmail. Live Mail is an app that can be accessed not only from your own computer, but you could also access your live account from anywhere there is a computer connected to the Internet, a hotel lobby, for example. This can give you some flexibility when it comes to accessing your mail when travelling. Live Mail can do more than just email but we will concentrate only on that feature here.

Opening Windows Live Mail

The Mail app is a very basic emailing system (see Figure 12.8). Desktop mail offers a far wider range of options. Search the Start menu to find the Windows Live Mail tile and activate it by clicking or tapping on the tile.

Figure 12.8

Sign in with the Live Mail address and password that your guardian angel set up for you. Click or tap in the Remember Me box (see Figure 12.9) to avoid having to do this every time you open up Live Mail. Click or tap on Sign In.

Figure 12.9

You should recognise many of the 'window' features shown in this view as many of the features work in similar ways to the WordPad window (Chapter 8), such as the Toolbar ribbons, sizing buttons and folder list. The difference is that these items are now specific to the Live Mail window.

You will see from Figure 12.10 that the Desktop version of Windows Live Mail is much more comprehensive than the Start screen version. Not only does it send and receive emails but it also incorporates a comprehensive toolbar ribbon, contacts list and a calendar. However, the folder sidebar, message list and selected message pane are still there and used in the same way as the Start screen app.

Fortunately, the method of sending emails is very similar to that used by the Start screen version.

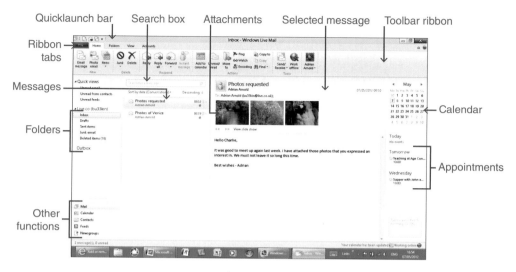

Figure 12.10

Sending an email in Desktop mode

Click or tap on the New icon in the lower-left part of the toolbar ribbon (see Figure 12.10) and a second window will appear (see Figure 12.11). This window should look familiar as it is very similar to the WordPad window we explored in Chapter 8.

Composing an email from Desktop mode follows the same procedure as Start screen mail:

1. Enter the recipient's email address in the address box.

2. Click or tap in the subject box and type a suitable heading.

3. Click or tap in the main message pane then type the message.

4. Click on the Attach icon if you want to add a file to the email.

5. Click on the Send button.

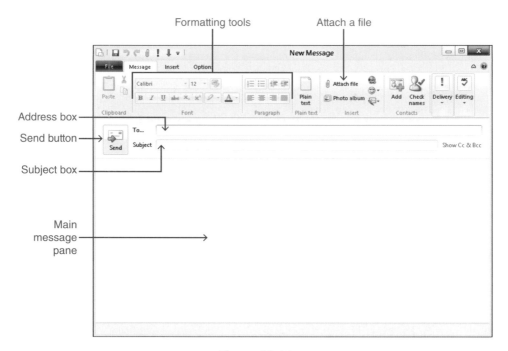

Formatting tools   Attach a file

Address box
Send button
Subject box
Main message pane

Figure 12.11

Receiving emails in Desktop mode

The Desktop email works in the same way as the Start screen Mail app. Provided you are connected to the Internet, every time you open Live Mail it will automatically download any waiting mail. It will check for new mail at regular intervals but click on the Send/Receive icon on the toolbar ribbon if you want to make a quick check for new mail.

In this chapter, we have tried to introduce you to the basics of emailing. There are many finer points to the emailing process but for now our advice is to practice. Experiment with the different toolbar ribbons; click on the Calendar option and make an appointment or play about with the Contacts options. You will make mistakes but the computer will not break down and you can always close the application, discard any mess you have created and make yourself a well-earned cup of tea.

The PCWisdom website offers tutorials and tips on the more advanced features of Live Mail in both Start screen and Desktop forms, as well as the use of other emailing applications. You will learn how to access this site in Chapter 13.

Summary

- Email is simply electronic mail.

- You can access your messages from both the Start screen Mail app and the Desktop Live Mail application.

- Make sure that you enter email addresses very accurately.

- Email addresses never include a space and always contain the @ symbol.

- Check your mail regularly.

- Files such as documents, photos and videos can be attached to email messages.

- Do not open any spam or junk mail.

- Any incomplete and unsent messages will be stored in the Drafts folder.

- Deleted mail is stored in the Delete items folder and is only lost forever when you empty this folder.

- Practice by sending emails to yourself.

Brain training

There may be more than one correct answer to the following questions.

1. Which of the following is a valid email address?

a) Martin jones@btInternet.com

b) Billjonesat.freemail.co.uk

c) Squid589c@gmail.com

d) Tom&jean<>@live.com

2. What happens if you type in an incorrect address?

a) Nothing

b) You will receive an email informing you of the problem

c) You will leave yourself vulnerable to unwanted mail

d) The message will not be sent

3. Which of these can you send as an attachment?

a) A video

b) An app

c) A scanned copy of a newspaper article

d) A computer program

4. How would you delete a message completely?

a) Highlight the message and hit the Delete key

b) Click the dustbin icon

c) Send the message to the Deleted items folder and then empty the folder

d) Use the right-click menu and select Delete Completely

Answers

Q1 – c   **Q2** – b

Q3 – a and c   **Q4** – c

Using the Internet

13

Equipment needed: A computer (laptop, tablet or desktop), Windows 8 operating system, monitor screen, preferably with touchscreen capability, keyboard and mouse or trackpad. You will also need an ISP Internet connection. A printer will be useful.

Skills needed: Keyboard and mouse (Chapter 1), knowledge of the Desktop interface (Chapter 3), familiarity with windows (Chapter 4), some experience with word processing (Chapter 8) and some idea of the Internet concept (Chapter 10).

This chapter leads you into the magical world of the Internet, using an application called a web browser. There are a number of browsers available and they all work in a similar way, but we will be using the most common one, Internet Explorer.

As we discussed in Chapter 10, many people use the terms Internet and World Wide Web synonymously but in fact, they are two different things: the Internet is a vast backbone of connections covering the globe by cable, satellite and radio links, while the World Wide Web (or simply the web or the Net) is the linked information stored on millions of computers (called servers) at the end of these connections. Servers may be huge (belonging, for example, to the CIA or UK government) or very simple computers in small offices. The computers run by your ISP and the government are servers; your desktop computer is not. The difference is that servers are fully automatic and permanently connected to the Internet for access by outsiders.

This is all rather academic and you do not have to worry about the nuances, because for our purposes, you can use the terms interchangeably and most people will understand what you mean.

Windows 8 offers two methods of accessing the Internet — using a Start screen app or a Desktop application. Both use Internet Explorer but in different forms, like the way Live Mail is used to send emails (see Chapter 12). If you have used previous Windows operating systems you will be familiar with the Desktop version.

Desktop Internet Explorer

Open the Desktop tile on the Start menu and look for the Internet Explorer icon on the main screen or the taskbar. Open the application by tapping or clicking on it. This will open Internet Explorer's Home Page (see Figure 13.1). In the case of Figure 13.2, the Home Page has been changed to the PCWisdom page. We will show you how to change the Internet Explorer Home Page later in the chapter but first we will examine its structure.

Figure 13.1

If you find that your page is not set out like the one in Figure 13.2, it may be that some of the toolbars are missing. To rectify this, move your mouse to the top of the screen in the blue area and then click the right mouse button. You can then select the toolbars you wish to display.

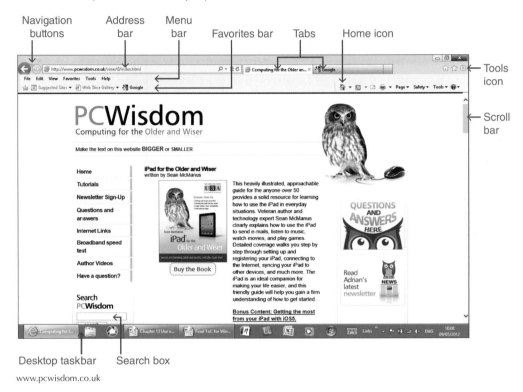

Figure 13.2

The Home Page

All websites are made up of pages of information that are presented to you through your web browser. Every website has a Home Page, which is the initial page you see when you open up a connection to a website on the Internet. The Home Page will allow you to access other pages through a series of links or buttons that you click upon. When you open a web browser like Internet Explorer, it will always take you to the Home Page of what is called the default website. Your Windows 8 computer will be set to go to a Microsoft website every time you connect to the Internet. This can be changed to a site of your choosing, Google for example.

The address bar

Every web page has an address, which usually starts with 'http://www.' or sometimes just 'http://'. Some are simple (**www.bbc.co.uk**) but others are much more complicated (**http://indepth.news.sky.com/InDepth/topic/David%20Cameron**). Don't worry, we will explain these long addresses a bit later. In fact, even if you just type in a 'www.' address, the computer will add the characters 'http://' or 'https://' for you. You do not have to worry about this it is simply the computer identifying the type of computer language that is needed to open the page.

Tap or click in the address bar. It will become highlighted in blue. As soon as you start typing in a new web address (known as a URL), the highlighting will disappear and your entry will be accepted.

Type **www.pcwisdom.co.uk** into the address bar and click or tap on the Enter key. This will bring up the main PCWisdom page, which supports the books in the Older and Wiser series.

Navigation buttons

Type **www.bbc.co.uk** into the address bar to bring up the main BBC page. You will notice that the left navigation button has turned blue. Click on this to return to the original Home Page. Now the right navigation button will be active and you can tap or click on this to return to the BBC page. If you have opened a series of pages you can navigate back and forward between the previously opened sites in this way.

The Home button

Tapping or clicking on this icon you will always return to your Home Page — a good reason to set your Home Page to one that you are likely to use on a regular basis.

Links

These are access points to other web pages (see Figure 13.1). Simply click or tap on the links. You can tell when the pointer is over a link because the pointer changes shape from a white pointer to a hand. A link may take you to a page within the website you are looking at or a different website altogether. You can always navigate your way back to the original page using the navigation buttons.

Click or tap on a few of the links available on the BBC page to open up other pages on the website.

Tabs bar

You can have two or more pages open at the same time. Hold down the Ctrl key at the same time as clicking on a link, and the new page will open in a new tab, shown to the right of the address bar. In Figure 13.2, two tabs are open — the PCWisdom site and a Google page.

Menu bar

Tapping or clicking on any of the options on the menu bar (see Figure 13.2) reveals a dropdown menu with a variety of options. Figure 13.3 shows the drop-down menu for the File option. This allows you to create a new tab, open a new window or print the web page, among other things.

The Edit menu allows to you to copy all or part of the web page to insert it into another document, the View menu changes the appearance of the window and the Tools menu offers opportunities to vary the actions of the Internet Explorer browser. The Help menu will often be able to answer your queries about the working of the application.

The Favorites menu is particularly useful.

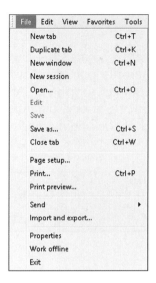

Figure 13.3

Favorites menu

You will come across pages that you find so informative that you want to return to them regularly. Instead of trying to remember their addresses, you can add them to your Favorites list. To do this:

1. Open the page that you want to save to your Favorites list.

2. Click or tap on Favorites on the menu bar.

3. Click or tap on the Add to Favorites option from the dropdown menu.

4. Type in a suitable descriptive name or leave the suggested name in place.

5. Click or tap on Add (see Figure 13.4).

The next time you want to return to the page, simply raise the Favorites menu again and you will see the site listed at the bottom of the menu. Tap or click on the link and bingo! The page leaps onto the screen.

Figure 13.4

Instead of saving a page to the Favorites list you can save it to the Favorites bar that runs across the top of the browser page window (see Figure 13.2) for even faster access.

Scrollbar

Many pages will be too long to be fully visible on the screen. With a touchscreen, you can drag the page up the screen by swiping a finger up the screen. In the absence of a touchscreen, you can use the scrollbar. Every scrollbar has a darker blue block lying within the bar. Clicking above or below the block will move the contents of the screen up or down, a page at a time. For more accurate scrolling, use the small arrow pointers at the top and bottom of the bar to move the screen contents one line at a time.

Setting your own Home Page

When you first take possession of a new computer, the Home Page may be set to the website of your ISP. These are rarely of much use beyond advertising their services so you need to change it to something more useful. Many beginners find that the Google Page is a much more helpful Home Page. To change your Home Page:

1. Open the page that you want to set as your Home Page (for example, type **www.google.co.uk** into the address bar and hit the Enter key).

2. Click on the Tools menu on the menu bar or click on the Tools icon.

3. Select Internet options from the dropdown menu.

4. The top option displays the address of your proposed new Home Page (see Figure 13.5).

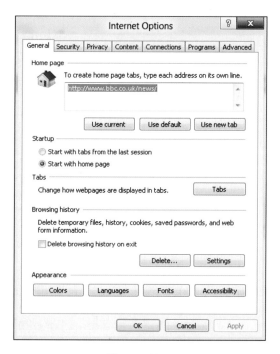

Figure 13.5

5. Simply click on Use Current and click on OK.

That's it. You have changed your Home Page. Congratulations.

Internet Explorer

This app uses the Internet Explorer web browser in a different way. From the Start screen, tap or click on the Internet Explorer tile to open the app (see Figure 13.6).

The advantage of apps is that they use the whole screen to display their function. The Internet Explorer app offers very similar command options to the Desktop application but they are found in different places on the screen.

Figure 13.6

The address bar lies at the bottom of the screen with the navigation buttons at either end (see Figure 13.7). They work in the same way as the Desktop version.

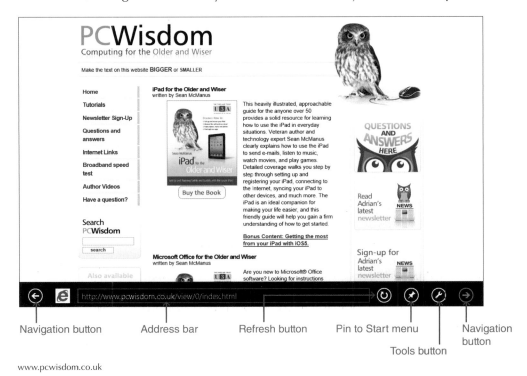

Figure 13.7

www.pcwisdom.co.uk

Refresh button

Websites are continually being updated. Some are updated only infrequently but others, such as news sites, alter minute by minute. Use the refresh button to load the very latest version of the web page.

Pin site menu

This is the new version of Favorites. When you find a page that you want to return to, tap or click on this button to pin the web page to the Start menu. Alternatively, you can set the web page as a favorite page within Internet Explorer.

Tools button

This button is very limited. It only offers the options of finding a word on a web page or opening the page in Desktop mode, where you will find a much more comprehensive set of tools.

Previously visited sites

This is a very neat function. Right-click on the screen or flick up from the lower edge and a series of thumbnails appears at the top of the screen showing the sites you have recently visited (see Figure 13.8). Windows 8 calls these thumbnails tabs (not to be confused with the tabs bar in the Desktop interface). To revisit one of these sites, simply click or tap on the thumbnail. If you are no longer interested in keeping the site as a tab, click or tap on the circled X in the top-right corner of the tab.

This chapter has given you some basic instructions about the use of Internet Explorer. You should now be able to raise a website using web addresses and find your way around various links — but that is only the start of your Internet experience. We will be developing the use of the Internet in the next few chapters.

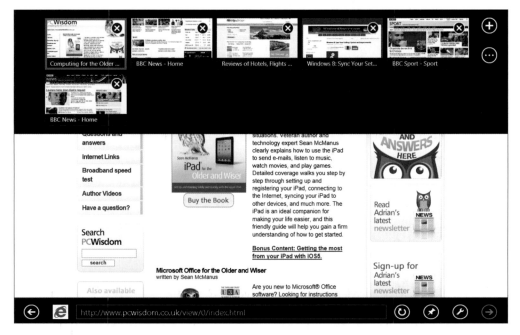

Figure 13.8

The Windows 8 version of Internet Explorer will develop over the next few years to include more features. These developments will be explained on the PCWisdom site (**www.pcwisdom.co.uk**) as they appear. Keep an eye out for future developments.

Summary

- The Internet browser Internet Explorer is available from both the Start and Desktop screens.

- The Desktop version is much more comprehensive.

- The Start screen version is more suited to touchscreen machines such as laptops and tablets.

- The arrow pointer changes to a hand when it is over a link.

- Use the navigation buttons to move back and forth between recently visited pages.

- Set your Home Page to a site that you will use most often.

- The Start screen does not use a Home Page but always opens at the last site you were viewing.

- Save useful sites to your Favorites.

- Open a page in a new tab window by holding down the Ctrl key when clicking on the link.

- Use a finger swipe or the scrollbar to move the page up and down the screen.

- In the Start screen, view previously opened sites by flicking a finger down from the top edge or right-click with the mouse.

Brain training

There may be more than one correct answer to the following questions.

1. Which of the following do you need to access the Internet?

a) An Internet Service Provider account

b) A computer connected by cable to the telephone point

c) A router

d) A powerful computer

2. What is a 'link' in the context of the Internet?

a) A memorised web page

b) A connection between one web page and another

c) An email sent from a web page

d) The connection between the computer and the Internet

3. How would you display a missing toolbar?

a) Press Ctrl+T

b) Use the Settings tile from the Start menu

c) Right-click on the toolbar area

d) Left-click on the title bar

4. How would you access previously visited sites?

a) Click or tap on Favorites in the Desktop browser menu bar

b) Swipe down from the top edge in the browser

c) Right-click on the browser page

d) You have to register the sites with your ISP

Answers

Q1 – a and c

Q2 – b

Q3 – c

Q4 – a, b and c

PART IV
Having Fun

Must you download so much stuff?

Exploring Windows apps

14

Equipment needed: A computer running Windows 8, monitor screen (preferably touchscreen) keyboard, mouse, Internet Explorer plus an Internet connection.

Skills needed: Comfortable with using the previously mentioned equipment (Chapter 1), Metro interface (Chapter 2), using Internet Explorer, and familiarity with Opening your first app (Chapter 7).

When Windows 8 is installed, a range of apps is already included in the Start menu. In previous chapters, we described how to use some of these apps. We looked at apps, such as Mail, the Desktop and Internet Explorer. If you glance at the Start screen, you can see that we have more to cover, including News, Sports, and Finance. In this chapter, we look further at some of the pre-installed apps and visit the Store where you can download a whole range of apps that you can then use to enrich your Windows 8 user experience.

About the Windows Store

The Store tile is present on your Start menu when Windows 8 is installed. You may have come across people talking about the App Store when they are discussing their Apple iPhones. The Windows Store is the Microsoft equivalent for

Windows 8. Keep in mind that several different operating systems are available for computers, each of which have their own apps. This one is purely for Microsoft, so you can't mix and match.

The Windows Store has been specially created for Windows 8 and even at this early stage in its life, a huge range of apps are available for download, including games, social, and entertainment, books, newspapers and travel.

You get an idea of what is available when you first click on the Store tile. Click on the tile, and the screen will display something similar to Figure 14.1.

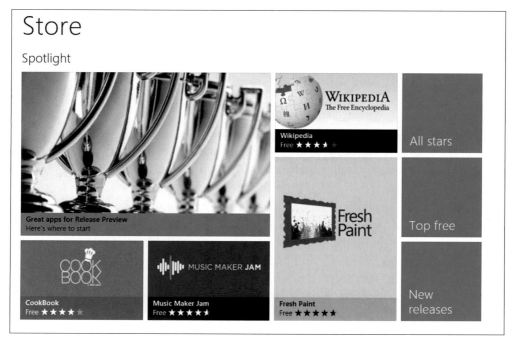

Figure 14.1

This will show the Home Page of the Windows Store with different apps that are available.

The Spotlight screen shows a summary of some of the apps available. If you look on the right side, you will see more apps that are available, all grouped into different categories. Moving your mouse will display the bar at the bottom of the screen. Moving this to the right will allow you to see the other categories.

You have so many options from which to choose, including:

- Games and Social
- Entertainment
- Photo
- Music & Video
- Sports
- Books
- Food & Dining

Refer to Figure 14.1. Notice the two green tiles on the right — All stars, Top free and New releases. Each category that you see when you drag the bar to the right has these tiles in common. Clicking on the green tiles opens up the world of apps.

We do not have enough pages in this book to cover all the apps in detail, but we will look at a couple and go through the process involved in downloading and using apps.

Drag the bar until you see the category News and Weather and then click on Top free. You can see some of the apps available for download in this section, as shown in Figure 14.2. Do you like newspapers? If so, this is the one for you.

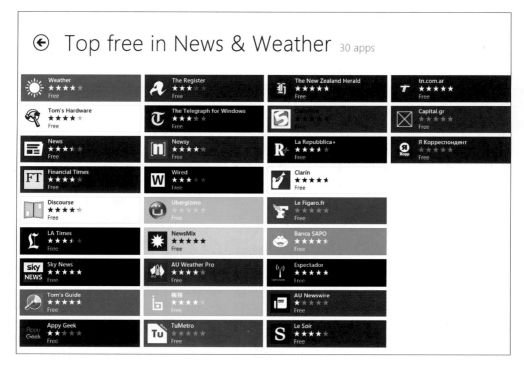

Figure 14.2

Click the circled arrow icon at the top left of the screen, and you return to the News and Weather category. Take a few minutes and browse some of the apps available. Click Top free to show only the free apps. Click New releases, and you will see any recent additions to the list of available apps. You will need to visit the New releases in your favourite categories periodically so that you can keep up with new arrivals. As Windows 8 matures, there will eventually be an app for whatever interests you — you just need to find it!

 Each app has a star rating. The number of stars is an indication of how popular or good an app may be.

Hundreds of apps are free, but this does not apply to all. You can think of a similar example: when we talk about newspapers, many free editions get delivered to your door, but you have to pay for your daily newspaper. We will revisit this topic a bit later in the chapter but at this stage let's enjoy free.

Downloading an app

Now that you have viewed the range of available apps, you probably have a list of those you wish to download. We'll download a newspaper app as an example, but of course the choice of which app to choose is up to you:

1. Go to the News and Weather category. You should see the available choices, as shown in Figure 14.2.

2. Click on the Financial Times tile. You are then presented with a screen similar to the screen shown in Figure 14.3.

   This screen tells you more about the app you have chosen. You may notice the popularity rating, but don't worry about this — everyone has different tastes.

3. Click the Install button if you accept the terms and conditions of the licence agreement.

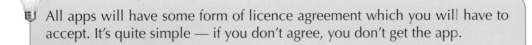

All apps will have some form of licence agreement which you will have to accept. It's quite simple — if you don't agree, you don't get the app.

How do you know the app is downloading? While the app installs, you will see purple dots moving along the top of the screen. If all is successful, the screen returns the Category display and a message will state that the Financial Times app is now installed as shown in Figure 14.4.

Figure 14.3

Figure 14.4

If you now return to the Start menu you can also see that the Financial Times app has been automatically pinned to the Start screen and is now available as shown in Figure 14.5. Congratulations, your first app is now installed! You can now download some more and watch your Start menu grow.

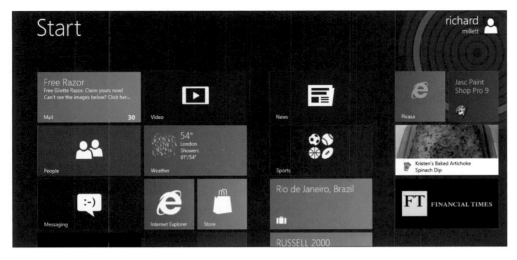

Figure 14.5

Free or paid

The newspaper app we installed in the previous section was a free app with the ability to choose a subscription, but that will not always be the case. Apps are split into three categories:

- Totally free to download and use: You incur no cost for downloading these apps.

- Pay once for continual use: You see a fixed price on the opening screen. You make a payment and then download the app just as you download a free app.

- Free trial then an ongoing subscription: You will get a free trial, typically 7 or 30 days, and then you will be required to sign up to a subscription if you wish to continue using this app.

Certain store categories show you a button at the top left where you can choose to display free or paid apps. Figure 14.6 shows you the dropdown menu.

How much do they cost? Some apps may cost literally pence, purely so the person who wrote it gets a return on his time. Others may cost a few pounds, depending upon their complexity. There is already a free star chart but a really fancy Astronomy app showing you interactive star maps may cost £2.50.

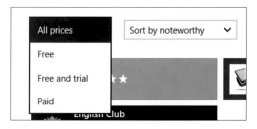

Figure 14.6

Paying for an app

How do you pay? For the one-off payments, you set up an account with the Microsoft Store by supplying them with your credit card details. The store then keeps these details and when you download an app it then applies a charge to your card. All you will have to do is enter your username and password to authenticate that you are the right person buying the app. Therefore, you don't have to keep providing your card details, but you do have to keep track of how much you spend. It's easy to get carried away and then you suddenly discover your apps have run up a bill of £50.

For some apps that require ongoing subscriptions, you need to set up an account with the provider of the app. Once again, something to keep track of.

Removing/unpinning an app

Suppose that you have downloaded a lot of apps and your Start menu has become too crowded.

To clean up your Start menu, you have some choices here. First, you can make some room by making the tile smaller. Notice that some tiles are square and some are double the size; you can make them smaller if you wish. With the Start menu displayed, move your mouse over the tile in question and click the right mouse button. A menu bar appears at the bottom, as shown in Figure 14.7.

Figure 14.7

The menu bar gives you different choices depending upon which tile you selected. Unpinning, Uninstalling, Making tile Smaller or Turning a Live Tile off are the choices you could have.

If you unpin an app, it disappears from the Start menu but is still accessible from the All Apps screen. Uninstalling does exactly that, so this is the one to use if you have no further need for an app. A Live Tile is one that is constantly changing, showing you updated or different information. This is where you can disable this feature.

Using apps

The way you use an app varies from one app to another. In the case of a newspaper, clicking upon the articles will display the content. In the cases of a cookery app, clicking on the menu shows you the contents.

Let's look at one of the preinstalled apps and do a little more with it. This time we will use People. This app is used to manage all your friends and contacts. It is a Windows version of your personal telephone directory, which is quite clever because it will actually add a lot of the contacts without you having to do anything. In Chapter 12, we looked at using email and if you think back, when we installed Windows 8 one of the things we had to do was set up an email address to log in to Windows. You may have used an email address that has been used previously, so when opening People for the first time you may get a surprise.

We open People by clicking on the tile on the Start menu. This will open a screen similar to Figure 14.8. This is where the surprise comes in because there may already be a list of contacts. When you add a mail or social networking account to Windows 8, it will go and find any contacts you have used with that account and automatically add them to this list. The more accounts you have, the more will be visible here.

On the left side of the screen, there is the option to add other accounts to your people. If you have other mail accounts or a social networking account on Facebook, for example, you can merge all your contacts from these services into the People app.

Figure 14.8

Let's say you want to add all your Facebook contacts into People. Click the Go to Settings and a dialog box appears on the right, as shown in Figure 14.8. Click on the Connect button below the Facebook icon on the right.

Figure 14.9 explains what will happen if you click the Connect button at the bottom of the screen. If you're happy with this click Connect, if not, click Cancel. If you connect, your list of contacts will increase.

Figure 14.9

Viewing contacts

You now have a list of all your contacts. Click on any of the contacts to see details about that individual.

We have clicked on David Wilson. You can see a summary of information, as shown in Figure 14.10, but this is the really clever bit. Click on the Map address and, hey presto, you now see the map of where he lives, as shown in Figure 14.11.

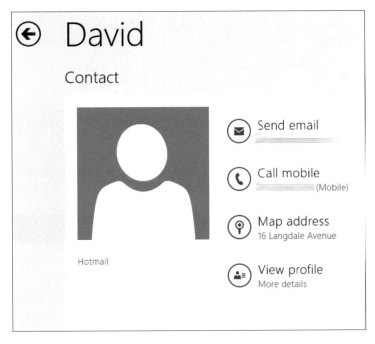

Figure 14.10

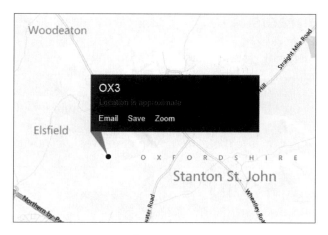

Figure 14.11

If you click on Send email, it will open up the mail application, so you can send a message or view a profile.

Clicking the right mouse button or swiping from the bottom of the screen produces a menu bar as shown in Figure 14.12.

Figure 14.12

Here you can change any of the details of a contact, delete the contact or even pin a contact to your Start menu, so you can access their details without even opening the People app.

Editing an app is a straightforward process. Simply click the Edit button and you are shown all the details of the contact similar to Figure 14.13. To make any changes, type the new details in the relevant box and then click the Save button at the bottom of the screen.

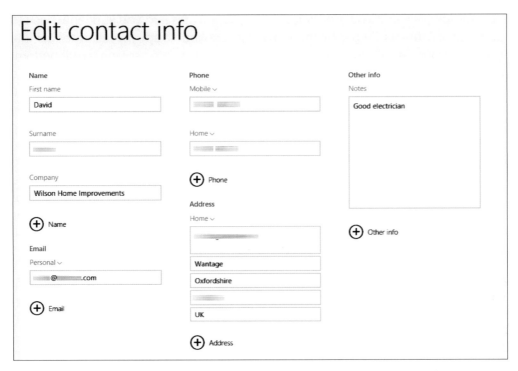

Figure 14.13

Moving between apps

Using the People app shows you that a lot of the apps you use are linked to each other: People and Maps, People and E-mail, and so on. This is one of the plus points of Windows so that you don't have to close one app to open another.

There will be, however, occasions when you are doing more than one thing at a time on your computer, after all, that is what they are designed to do.

For example, say that you are running a cookbook app and you suddenly wish to check on a contact. You can minimize the cookbook app by using either the mouse or your finger and swiping from the top centre of the screen to the bottom. You will know when you are in the right place to do this because the mouse pointer will change from an arrow to a hand. Doing this will take you back to the Start screen, and you can then click on the People tile to check your contact. This app will then open. There are two ways of recovering the cookbook app. One we have discussed before — to view all open apps, you move the mouse to the top-left corner of the screen then move it down the left edge to display a view of all the open apps. Another way is to hold the Alt and the Tab key down at the same time. Doing this displays all the apps you currently have running. Simple click or touch the app to which you wish to return. One of the things about Windows is that there is usually more than one way of carrying out a particular function. Use the one that suits you, because there is no right or wrong way.

Figure 14.14 shows the Alt and Tab keys pressed at the same time displaying eight different apps running. When you minimize an app, it runs in the background, so it is still alive but it isn't actually doing anything until you bring it back to the main screen.

Figure 14.14

PCWisdom

In this section, you have looked at using apps but throughout the book I have covered a wide range of topics. If you find that you need additional help on some of these topics, you can go to the PC Wisdom website. This website is designed as a companion site to the *Older and Wiser* series of books. You can access it by using the web address **www.pcwisdom.co.uk** where you will find a lot of useful information. This book cannot cover the full capabilities of Windows 8, especially because it will evolve over the first few years. PC Wisdom will be able to keep you up to date with future developments as they come on stream.

It is a useful website on which to practice your Internet browsing. Simply click or tap on the links and use the navigation buttons to explore the site. Unless you choose to buy one of the books listed on the site, you will incur no charges when browsing the site.

On the website, you'll find tutorials to help you with some of the more advanced uses of the system, articles on new apps as they appear, and the opportunity to put any questions — however silly they may sound — to Adrian as well as make a request to receive Adrian's newsletters. The newsletters are issued every two months and sent directly to your email address. Any suggestions for additional content are very welcome.

The site also gives details of the other books in the *Older and Wiser* series as well as a useful broadband speed calculator if you want to find out your personal broadband connection.

Summary

- Apps are opened from the Start screen.

- Many apps are pre-installed but others can be downloaded from the store.

- Apps in the Store are grouped in categories.

- Some apps are free to download and use, others may require payment or subscription.

- Many of the apps are linked so that you can open one from inside another to view additional information.

- Apps and contacts can be pinned or removed from the Start menu by choice.

- The People app can be used from a central location for all contacts from multiple email accounts.

- Apps are minimized by swiping from the top of the screen to the bottom.

- There are two ways of moving between apps.

Brain training

There may be more than one correct answer to the following questions:

1. Which apps can we add to our computer?

    a) Apps from the Windows store

    b) Apps from the Apple store

    c) Any App from any store

    d) Only free apps

2. How many apps can you have on the Start menu?

    a) 32

    b) 48

    c) 64

    d) As many as you like

3. How do you remove an app completely?

    a) Drag the tile and drop in the dustbin

    b) Right-click the app and select unpin

    c) Right-click the app and select Uninstall

    d) Right-click the app and turn Live Tile off

4. How can you move between apps?

    a) Use the Alt and Ctrl keys together

    b) Use the Alt and Tab keys together

    c) Move the mouse to the top left of the screen and then drag down

    d) Move the mouse to the bottom left of the screen and drag up

Answers

Q1 – a   **Q2** – d

Q3 – c   **Q4** – b and c

Installing software

15

Equipment needed: A computer, Windows 8, an ISP subscription, Internet Explorer 10, screen, keyboard and mouse or trackpad. A printer will be very useful.

Skills needed: Screen, keyboard, mouse and trackpad (Chapter 1), Start screen and Desktop interfaces (Chapters 2 and 3), familiarity with the Internet (Chapter 13) and navigating the system (Chapter 5).

There are two common ways in which you can install additional programs onto your computer — by using a program disc or by downloading programs from the Internet. In this chapter, we explain both methods. The prospect of installing a new program may seem daunting at first but, if you follow the instructions below, you will find that the process is largely automatic. Simply follow the recommended actions.

Installing a program from a disc

Your computer will come with some apps already loaded onto it. In previous chapters, we used some of these programs to learn the basics of operating a computer, but there is a huge difference in being able to operate a computer and being able to use it to its potential. To do this, you need to install additional applications or programs.

For example, you have already learned how to type letters and other documents using WordPad, a very basic word processing program. As you progress, you will probably find that WordPad does not possess the capabilities that you require as your interest and expertise develops. You may then decide to invest in a more comprehensive program, such as its big brother, Microsoft Word. In the field of digital photography, you may be content to use the freely available Windows Photo Gallery, but if you want to develop computing photography as a hobby, you are going to need a more comprehensive program, such as Photoshop Elements.

> It is a good idea to close down all open programs before installing a new one. This will prevent any conflicts from arising during the installation process.

Installing a program from a disc

In this example, we walk you through the process of installing the Photoshop Elements application, or program. First, you need to find the CD/DVD tray that lies at the front of a desktop machine or to one side of a laptop. To open the disc tray, push the edge in towards the body of the machine, and the tray will slide out of its own accord. The disc is normally contained in a plastic container called a *jewel box* and, because some programs cost upwards of £600, they are aptly named. Slide the disc onto the tray with the printed side uppermost and shiny side down. With a large desktop machine, the disc should sit loosely in the tray, but with a laptop you click the disc into the tray before gently pushing the tray back into place. Within a few seconds, you will hear a whirring sound and the light on the DVD tray will begin to flicker.

A small box appears in the top-right corner of the screen, inviting you to tap or click on it to view the options, as shown in Figure 15.1.

Viewing the option opens a small window that includes the option to **Run Setup exe.** (see Figure 15.2).

Figure 15.1

Figure 15.2

Click on that option, and you are asked whether you trust the contents of the disc. You can confidently accept discs from respected program manufacturers, such as Microsoft, Adobe and Norton but beware of copied or pirated discs that may contain viruses or other malware.

The licence for the program, shown in Figure 15.3, appears on the next screen, which you need to accept. This basically says that you agree not to allow other people to use the program or copy it in any way that breaches the company's copyright. Depending on the program in question, you may see a small box that you need to click in order to accept the terms of the licence before you can continue with the installation.

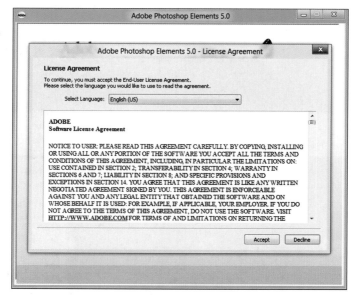

Figure 15.3

There will follow a number of windows asking you to accept various selections suggested by the installation process. At some point, you will be asked for the *product key* or serial number, which is normally found on the jewel box or within the instruction manual (see Figure 15.4).

Product keys come in a variety of forms. They may be a continuous block of alphanumeric characters or be split into blocks. Make sure that you enter the characters accurately, paying attention to upper and lowercase characters. If you make a mistake, the installation program will almost certainly notify you and refuse to continue with the installation process until the correct key is entered.

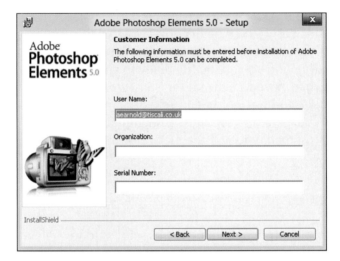

Figure 15.4

Depending on the individual program, you may be asked a number of other questions most of which will show a recommended option. The recommended options are fine for nearly all users, so until you become more accomplished, just follow the instructions that will usually consist of clicking the Next option, and the program will start to load. The progress of the installation is often shown by a bar, which gradually fills up — like a horizontal thermometer.

The product key is a very important piece of information, so do not throw the packaging away. The product key may be printed on the box or the CD Jewel case. You will need it if you have to re-install the program onto a new computer.

Eventually the installation will complete successfully, and you may be asked some questions, including if you want to have a Desktop shortcut, whether you to start the program immediately, and whether you are agreeable for the company to collect user statistics from your computer. We would opt out of the last option. Click on the Finish button, and you are nearly ready to go. For the more expensive programs, you may then have to activate the software. This tells the vendor that the software is genuine and has not been pirated. This process takes place over the Internet and only takes a few seconds. Congratulations! You are now done and legal. On the Start screen, you will see the application tile pinned to the right end of the block of tiles.

Copyright issues

It is a crime to install a program that you have not paid for unless it is specifically labeled as free software. Free software? Is that the same as a free lunch? Definitely not, and we will be discussing the subject of the different types of software programs in a moment. Here's an example relating to the crime of software piracy. Say that a friend at work, or one of your children, learns that you are looking for a simple home accounting program. They may have a program disc at home that would suit your requirements. "No problem," they say. "I'll pop round and install it for you on Saturday morning." How kind, how considerate — how criminal. You are both committing an act of software theft or piracy. Do you remember the licence contract you accepted without a second thought when installing the program? You agreed, by accepting that contract, not to "copy, share, loan or sell" and various other legal terms meaning the same thing not to do what you have arranged to do on that Saturday morning. For this reason, software has to be activated, to ensure that a single copy is not being used on more than one computer.

Lots of people do break the licencing contract — akin to travelling at 50mph in a 30mph traffic zone — and they get away with it. That does not mean it is right. Leave the matter to your own moral judgement.

Types of software

There are basically three types of software. These applications are run by the computer, as opposed to hardware such as the computer itself, the screen, printers, scanners, disc drives and the other tangible goods that make up a computing system.

Commercial software

Commercial software is purchased from computing outlets or on the web for which you pay the full price. Examples of such software include the Microsoft Word program for word processing, Adobe's Photoshop programs for photo editing and the Family Tree Maker program used by genealogists. When you buy these programs, you are paying for permission to use the program on your own personal computers, and you are entitled to a varying degree of support in the event of something going wrong. Commercial software forms the bulk of programs used on a computer.

Freeware software

We mentioned this concept earlier in the chapter, and you are entitled to think that we were pulling your leg. After all, there is no such thing as a free lunch in this world, but in this case, you can really dine for free and the menus can be very appetising. How can this be?

There are a variety of reasons. First, in spite of this age of cynical materialism, many altruistic people simply enjoy creating good programs for the fun of it as well as to gain a sense of community with other like-minded souls. Freeware also places the programmer's work in the shop window of the commercial operators. These companies often employ programmers on a freelance basis to solve particular problems they may be having with their own products. Freeware can also be viewed as apprentice's work like that of an aspiring silversmith. Last but not least, there are many individuals and organisations that object to the monopolies held by multinational software developers and wish to offer alternatives to expensive commercial programs.

Many freeware programs are of the highest quality and invaluable to many computer users. In fact, we walk you through how to load a free photo editing application called Picasa in this chapter, which allows you to catalogue and manipulate digital images. Other examples of freeware programs are the Open Office — a suite of programs that offers a combination of word processor, spreadsheet, presentation and database facilities among others and Google Earth, which offers satellite viewing of most locations on this planet of ours — even down to street addresses.

Shareware programs

Shareware is a kind of halfway house between the full retail product and the freeware alternative. These programs may be free to download and install, but the length of time they can be used after installation is limited. They may be cut-down versions of commercial programs but which prevent the use of certain aspects of the program until a small fee has been paid to the programmer. These fees are rarely more than £30 or $50 and can be very good value for money. For example, maybe you would like to have a particular type of program on your computer, such as a web page designer or home finance software but you don't know which one suits you best. Very often you can download a trial shareware version and play around with it for a few weeks to test its capabilities before committing yourself to the full product. Most trial software will allow you to run the program for up to 30 days. At the end of this period, the program will stop working and you will get a pop-up reminder. If you now purchase the product, all you buy is the licence key, you already have the software so you do not need to reinstall the program.

Installing a program from the Internet

Many applications or programs can be downloaded directly from the Internet. They may be commercial, shareware or freeware. If you want to download a commercial program you will need a debit or credit card to pay for the program. You will then receive an email message confirming your purchase and providing you with the necessary product key or serial number. Make a record of this number and keep it safe.

Downloading and installing Picasa

Picasa is one of those invaluable freeware programs from the Google stable of thoroughbreds that allows you to catalogue and sort your photographs as well as apply some quite sophisticated improvements to your digital images. Because we do not have a disc containing the program, we need to download it from the web by taking the following steps:

1. Close any programs you may have running on the taskbar at the bottom of the screen.

2. Connect to the Internet, launch Internet Explorer and call up the Google home page at **www.google.co.uk**.

3. At the right end of the menu options, click on the More link and then click on the Even more link from the dropdown menu, which brings you to the page looking like Figure 15.5.

Reproduced by permission of Google™ ©2012

Figure 15.5

4. And you thought that Google was just a search engine, didn't you? This page shows how much more Google can do than search the web. The program that

we are interested in is Picasa in the right column under Communicate, Show and Share. Click on the Picasa icon.

5. You could take time out here to find out a bit more about Picasa by following a few of the links on this page but, eventually, we want you to click on Download Picasa (Figure 15.6).

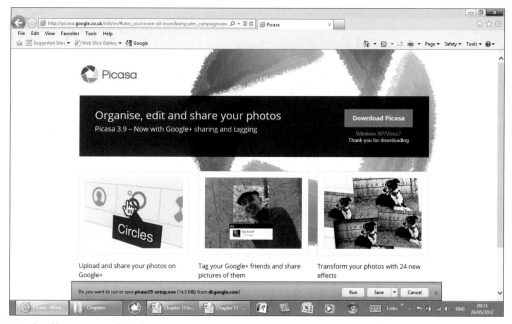

Reproduced by permission of Google™ ©2012

Figure 15.6

6. You will be asked whether you want to save or run the program after it is downloaded. We suggest that you choose to run it. The computer will suggest a location in which to save the program. Accept this suggestion by tapping or clicking on OK.

7. The program should then start to download to your computer within a few seconds. The process takes a varying length of time depending upon the speed of your Internet but it should take no longer than five minutes.

8. You will be asked whether you are prepared to accept the download from Google to which the answer is yes. The installation begins. You must agree to the licence as discussed previously and then select Install.

9. The setup program finishes by installing a Picasa icon on your Start screen (see Figure 15.7).

Figure 15.7

10. At the end of the installation, you will be offered a number of options, such as placing an icon on the desktop or running the program immediately. We suggest that you do not opt to start the program immediately because this exercise has been about downloading and installing programs from the web and, at this stage, you probably do not have many images stored on the computer. After you have loaded some photos, you can start Picasa, which will collect and catalogue all the photos on the computer. Having made your selection of the options by deselecting the ones you don't want, simply click Finish.

That's it! You have just downloaded and installed your first program from the web.

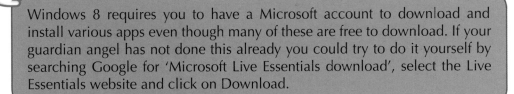

Windows 8 requires you to have a Microsoft account to download and install various apps even though many of these are free to download. If your guardian angel has not done this already you could try to do it yourself by searching Google for 'Microsoft Live Essentials download', select the Live Essentials website and click on Download.

Summary

● Applications or programs can be installed from a disc or directly from the Internet.

● Close down open programs before installing a new one.

● Insert the program disc with the printed side up.

● Choose the default or 'recommended' options during the installation process.

● Once you have started the installation, leave the computer alone to do its work.

● Program keys and serial numbers are valuable. Store them safely.

● Installing a program is a relatively simple operation if you follow the screen instructions.

● Make sure that you answer all the questions asked during the installation process so that you can continue to the next stage

● There are three basic types of software — commercial, shareware and freeware.

● Freeware does not necessarily mean sub-standard programs.

● Shareware can often give you a feel for a program before you commit yourself to buying.

● If an Accept option is unavailable, it is because you have not selected the acceptance box.

● The installed program appears as a tile at the right end of the Start menu.

Brain training

There may be more than one correct answer to these questions.

1. When loading a disc which side should face down?

a) The printed side

b) The shiny side

c) It does not matter. The DVD reader scans both sides.

d) The side with a printed number round the central hole.

2. What is shareware?

a) Programs that analyse the stock markets

b) Programs bought by people who share the cost

c) Cut-down or time limited programs

d) Software for Apple Mac computers

3. What is a product key?

a) A code that allows you to use a program

b) A plastic tool that is used to get the disc out of its case

c) A security device on the back of a computer

d) An advertising logo

4. What do software copyrights prevent you from doing?

a) Allowing a friend to install it on his machine

b) Selling it to a third party

c) Installing it on a replacement computer that you buy second is the correct term here. It is possible to transfer a licence to a replacement computer.

d) Copying the contents onto another disc

Answers

Q1 – b

Q3 – a

Q2 – c

Q4 – a, b and d

Search engines

16

Equipment needed: A computer, Windows 8, a subscription with an ISP, Internet Explorer 10, screen, keyboard and mouse or trackpad. A printer will be very useful.

Skills needed: Screen, keyboard, mouse and trackpad (Chapter 1), Start screen interface (Chapter 2), Desktop interface (Chapter 3) and use of Internet Explorer 10 (Chapter 13).

We have already looked at a few websites, but you will want to explore your own interests on the web. So how do you find what you are looking for? By using a search engine.

Search engines use highly sophisticated programming to search the vast Internet network. They constantly send out 'spiders' to trawl the web for the latest websites, and the information they gather is then available for anyone to use.

There are a number of search engines, such as Ask (**www.ask.com**), Yahoo! (**www.yahoo.com**) and Bing (**www.bing.com**) but the undisputed leader in the field is Google. There are many international versions of this search engine but the two designed for the English-speaking world are **www.google.com** (American) and **www.google.co.uk** (English). There are minor differences between the two, so we are going to stick with the Google UK version.

In this chapter, we will be asking you to enter various words into a search box. When we ask you to enter, for example, 'sheffield university', you should omit the quote marks when you type in the text.

Google

Even 'non-computerate' people have probably heard the term 'to google' but might not know what it means. It is simply a method of searching the web for information. The Google Home Page, shown in Figure 16.1, is a classic example of simplicity combined with function. In its basic form, you simply have to type a few key words relevant to your enquiry into the search box and click on Google Search. For example, if you are interested in Egyptian mosques, type 'egypt mosque' into the search box and press the Enter key or click on Google Search.

Reproduced by permission of Google™ ©2012

Figure 16.1

You do not have to capitalise words in the search box. Even typing in 'LoNDoN' will find pages relevant to the capital. You may also have noticed that we use the singular form of the words rather than the plural because the search for the singular will always find the plural but not the other way round.

A glance at the search results page in Figure 16.2 shows that it has found more than 18 million pages in less than a second. This gives some idea of the enormity of the web and how quickly the Google search engine performs its tasks. Fortunately, Google organises the search results in order of likely interest with the most useful websites at the top of the list. Many search words activate commercial links to allied subjects. It is these links, listed in a column to the right of the search results and paid for by the various companies, that gather the revenue for the Google company.

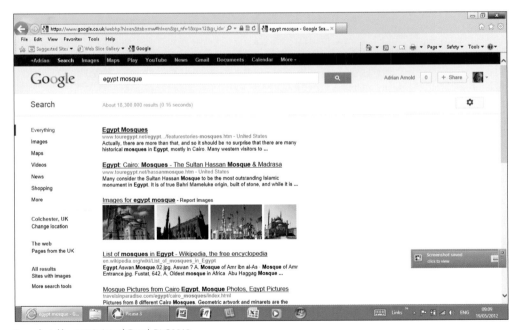

Reproduced by permission of Google™ ©2012

Figure 16.2

Let us take a look at the search result in Figure 16.3. The first blue line of text is the link to this particular site, reviews of The Mosque of Ibn Tulun. Clicking on this line will take you to the website. The green text gives the web address (URL) of the site. The line of stars indicates that this is a review site and that the attraction has an overall rating of four-and-a-half stars out of five. The following figure shows the first few lines of text from the website, to give you further information.

Reproduced by permission of Google™ ©2012

Figure 16.3

We could refine the search by adding further words to the search box. If we added the word 'alexandria' to the search terms (leaving the word 'egypt' in the search box as well, to differentiate Alexandria in Egypt from the Alexandrias in Vermont and Australia), we would reduce the number of 'hits' from 18 million to 2 million. We could refine the search still further by adding the word 'hotel' to the search box. This finds only 900,000 pages that include all four words.

Something that tends to confuse beginners is the difference between the window address bar and the Google search box. If you know the correct web address (or URL) of the site, type it into the address bar. But if you are searching for websites and do not have a particular address, type the relevant search words in the search box.

Modifying characters

You can further refine your searches by using modifying characters. For instance, you might be looking for articles on Sheffield Hallam University. Entering those three words in the search box will produce a result but a number of these sites will refer to Sheffield United and Sheffield Wednesday football teams, which aren't relevant to your search. You can eliminate references to these teams by entering any terms in the search box you don't want to be included, with a minus sign before them ('-united -wednesday'). This tells Google to ignore these specific terms and results in more accurate search results.

Another characteristic of search engines is that they tend to ignore certain small words such as 'and' and 'the', as well as numbers. This means that a search for the film *Rocky III* results in references to all the *Rocky* films. To make sure the search includes such numbers or words, add a plus sign in front of the term ('rocky +3').

At the beginning of this chapter we asked you to exclude any quote marks from your search word. But there are some cases where quote marks are invaluable. This is when you are searching for a specific phrase. Let us imagine that you have forgotten the title of the theme song of the film, *The Thomas Crown Affair*. However, you do remember that the lyric contains the line "circles that you find". If you searched for 'circles that you find' as separate words, Google would almost certainly ignore the words 'that' and 'you' and simply search for sites containing the words 'circle' and 'find', which would result in 965 million results, none of which would be of any value whatsoever. The trick here is to get Google to search for the specific phrase by using double quotation marks ("circles of your mind"). This reduces the number to 322,000, all of which are relevant to your enquiry and allow you quickly to establish that the song is called "Windmills of your Mind".

You can refine your search by using the Advanced Search Settings option from the Tools icon, which is the symbol that looks like a cogwheel at the right of the search options bar.

Definitions

You can also use Google to find definitions, calculate currencies and perform simple calculator tasks.

To get a dictionary definition of the word 'zeitgeist', type in 'define: zeitgeist' and you will get a list of definitions from various web dictionaries. Note that we used a colon to separate the two words in this case.

You may be about to take a holiday in Tokyo and have researched a number of guided tours around the city. Unfortunately, these tours are priced in the local currency, yen. Are they expensive or good value for money? Go to the main Google page and type in '300 yen in pounds'. The answer (£2.47 at today's rate) is displayed almost immediately, using the most current exchange rate.

Other Google search services

Looking back at Figure 16.1, you will notice that Google does not restrict itself to searches of websites but will also find images, maps, videos and news items. Let us say you would like to know more about the green woodpecker. Using those two words in the search box brings up a million websites but clicking on the Images link in the top-left corner will produce 194,000 pictures. The Video link lists 1,400 video clips of the bird in flight and even the Maps link finds Milton Green, Woodpecker Drive!

Images

Click on the Images link. By using the refining facilities listed down the left side (see Figure 16.4), you can restrict the image search to particular sizes and formats. Save these images to your computer by right-clicking on a picture, choosing the option to Save Image As from the dropdown menu and selecting the folder in which you want to save the file.

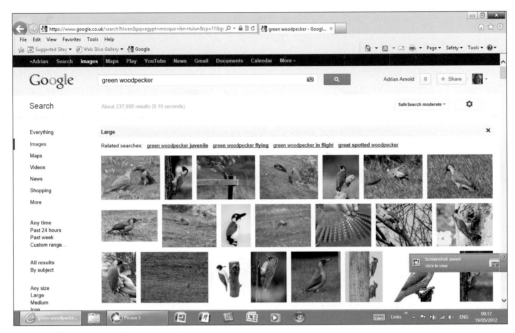

Figure 16.4

Videos

Google recently acquired the YouTube website (**www.youtube.com**), which offers a vast library of videos ranging from music and comedy to invaluable tutorials on almost any subject under the sun, from computer programs such as Microsoft Word and Excel to ballroom dancing, Tai Chi, embroidery and home plumbing. It is often much easier to learn a skill when it is demonstrated rather than trying to learn from a book.

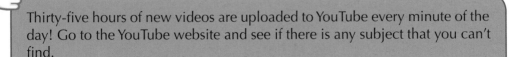

Thirty-five hours of new videos are uploaded to YouTube every minute of the day! Go to the YouTube website and see if there is any subject that you can't find.

Play videos by clicking on the arrow in the bottom-left corner (see Figure 16.5). This is a 'toggle' switch, which alternates between Play and Pause. The Pause function is shown by two vertical lines instead of the arrow symbol. The white ball travelling from left to right above the toolbar shows the progress of the video clip. You can 'drag' the ball back to the left to rewind the video to an earlier point or fast forward it by dragging it to the right. (This does not work until the whole video has been downloaded.)

Video Source: Adrian Arnold. © 2012 YouTube, LLC

Figure 16.5

Click on the Full screen icon at the bottom right to enlarge the picture. Press the Esc key to return to the smaller screen. These controls are normally found on any video found on the Internet.

You will need to keep your Flash player up to date to play these films accurately. Your computer may have had Adobe Flash Player already installed on it when you bought it but you still need to keep it up to date. You will occasionally be presented with a small window asking if you want to update the program. Accept the offer and follow the simple instructions. If Adobe Flash Player has not been installed, why not use Google to find it? Simply type 'adobe flash' into the search box and Google will point you to the right place to download Flash.

Maps

You can find maps of almost anywhere on Earth using the Maps option. Click on Maps then type an address or postcode into the search box. If there are alternatives, they will be listed below the box for you to choose the correct destination. 'Queens Road, Adelaide' will take you to South Australia while 'Agnes Road, W3' will land you in west London.

You can replace the resulting map with a satellite view of the area or see the location on the Google Earth map (see Figure 16.6). There are further options to view the local public transport facilities, current traffic density and weather. Choosing the Get Directions option to get directions from one site to another — Google will even tell you the anticipated driving time of the journey.

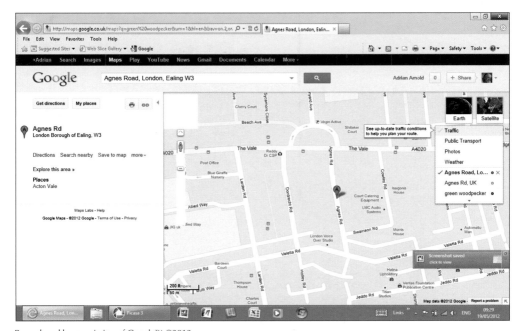

Reproduced by permission of Google™ ©2012

Figure 16.6

Google Maps can be viewed as a road atlas or as a satellite view. Try zooming in on your own house.

Other Google services

Google may be the market leader in the search engine field but it does much more than just search the web. Clicking on the word 'More' at the right of the search options will offer a huge range of other services (see Figure 16.7). These include translation of text from one language to another, online shopping, free email accounts, image adjustment and cataloguing facilities as well as opportunities to store your personal documents on the web for later retrieval should you happen to be using a computer in a different part of the world. This is known as cloud computing (see Chapter 11), which will play an increasing role in computing over the next few years.

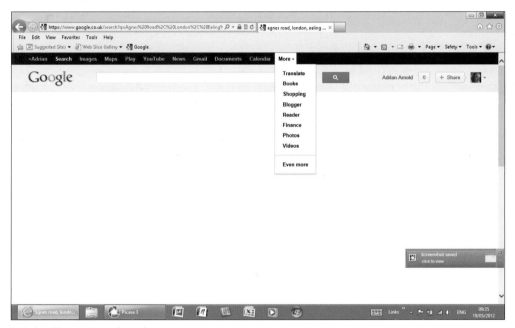

Reproduced by permission of Google™ ©2012

Figure 16.7

Click on Even More at the bottom of the menu to display the full range of Google services. If you want to explore the possibilities of the various Google programs, we recommend the Help facility at **www.google.com/help**.

More than 620 million people visit Google.com every day. Almost half of all Google products are still in development. There are more than 140 million Google mail users. Google processes 20 petabytes of information daily. A petabyte equals 1,000 terabytes, each of which contains 1,000 gigabytes. These figures are beyond the comprehension of the average mind!

Alternative search engines

Google is dominant in the search engine field but there are many others available on the Internet. If Google cannot find what you are looking for, try Bing (**www.bing.com**) or Yahoo! (**www.yahoo.com**). They both work in similar ways to Google but may produce the result you are looking for. Bing, Microsoft's latest venture into the search engine field, tries to be more intuitive than Google by offering helpful suggestions relevant to your search in a column down the left side of the results. It also offers searches of images, videos and more detailed maps.

The final search engine we want to mention is Ask (**www.ask.com**). You may find this tool easier to use if you have a specific question such as "How old was Danny Kaye when he died?"

Summary

- The web is a vast reference library, advice centre, classroom and travel guide.

- Search engines are websites that search the web.

- Search words are not case-sensitive — it doesn't matter if you use lowercase or capital letters.

- Use the address box for web addresses and the search box for search terms.

- Google is the market leader in search engine technology and also offers a huge range of other tools.

- Do not rely on just one search engine.

- Use quote marks when searching for phrases.

- Use the plus and minus operators to refine your search.

- Use video tutorials to expand your skills.

Brain training

There may be more than one correct answer to the following questions.

1. **Which of the following is provided by Google?**

   a) A word processor

   b) An email address

   c) A world atlas

   d) A translation facility

2. **Which of the following are valid search terms?**

   a) bOsTOn

   b) "mary had a little lamb"

   c) Radio +1

   d) johndoe@gmail.com

3. **What is YouTube?**

   a) A plumbing device

   b) An underwater cable that is part of the Internet

   c) A vast library of video clips

   d) A search engine

4. **How would you limit your search to a particular phrase?**

   a) Include the word 'phrase' in your search words

   b) Enclose the words in brackets

   c) Use the word 'define' with a colon

   d) Enclose the words with quotation marks

Answers

Q1 – b, c, and d

Q3 – c

Q2 – a, b and c

Q4 – d

Shopping online

17

Equipment needed: A computer with screen, keyboard and mouse; an Internet connection; an ISP account; Windows 8 operating system; a credit or debit card and a printer.

Skills needed: Keyboard and mouse (Chapter 1), Windows 8 screens (Chapters 2 and 3), emailing (Chapter 12), knowledge of using the Internet browser (Chapter 13) and the ability to search the web (Chapter 16).

There are huge bargains to be found on the web. However, you should be aware that there are some cowboys out there but you can save a lot of money by shopping online by taking simple precautions and using your common sense. Remember, if something sounds too good to be true then it almost certainly is.

Economics of the web

Why are goods often so much cheaper on the web than they are in the high street? It is all a matter of overheads:

- A business selling on the web does not have to pay rents, rates, maintenance and insurance on multiple premises.
- The number of staff needed is minimal compared with standard retail outlets.

- There is no need to stock showrooms with goods that quickly become 'shop soiled'.
- Warehouses can be sited on industrial estates with good transport links and low overheads.
- Automated ordering by computer reduces the need for expensive sales staff.

Shopping on the web does have its disadvantages, however:

- It is difficult to assess the quality of the goods without seeing them.
- Postage and carriage costs may increase the cost of goods, cancelling out any savings you may make on the sale price.
- There is no opportunity to negotiate over the price.
- It can be difficult to compare brands if you have to rely on images and a written specification.
- You lose the benefit of human contact.
- You may have to pay the costs of returning any unwanted goods.

Often the best way is to take advantage of both worlds by viewing and comparing the goods in the retail outlets and then making your purchase on the web. Please do not be misled into believing that everything on the web is cheaper. You may see a reduced sale item in a catalogue and then try to order the item on the web, only to find that it is only offered at the original pre-sale price, and the sale price is only available if you buy in-store or by mail order. Local travel agents will often have bargain deals in the shop window that only last for a short period of time and do not appear on their parent company's website.

Financial security

Security is an understandable source of anxiety for the beginner, so we would like to give you a little reassurance here — you are far more likely to lose your credit card details by accidentally leaving your purse or wallet in the local coffee shop or filling station forecourt than by entering the card details into a secure web page. Any self-respecting commercial website employs sophisticated encryption programs to guard against the possibility of your financial details being intercepted. We will discuss the signs of an encrypted web page later.

Your most effective defence against computer fraud is simple common sense. If you decide to buy a 'genuine' Rolex watch or invest in some obscure shares offering 'guaranteed' profit on the basis of an unexpected email from Russia, then I am afraid you deserve everything that happens to your bank account. We discussed the perils of junk email, or 'spam', in Chapter 12 but, to reinforce the message, *never* reply to any suspicious or unexpected email messages.

Bear in mind that credit card transactions are better protected than those using a debit card. If anything goes wrong with the transaction, you are usually covered by the insurance offered by credit card companies. This is why many companies charge a small fee for the use of credit cards — it pays for the insurance cover of your purchase.

A practice purchase

Maybe you are fed up with cold damp towels, so you decide to buy a towel radiator. This is quite a large item so it would be useful to buy it on the Internet and get it delivered. You have heard good reports about B&Q who specialise in do-it-yourself projects and have a good range of bathroom accessories so you want to check out their website. Using the B&Q website does not imply a recommendation to use this company. We are only using their website as an example. There are other websites, such as Homebase or Screwfix that also have good reputations.

What is the web address of B&Q? You could try various names, such as **www.b&q.com** or **www.b&q.co.uk** but they do not produce a result, so it must be something else. Open up the Google search engine and search for B&Q. This will help find the correct site and, lo and behold, the correct address for B&Q is actually **www.diy.com**. If in doubt, always use a search engine.

Figure 17.1 shows the Home Page of the B&Q website. We have clicked on the Rooms category, which has produced a dropdown menu that includes heating and radiators. We had to scroll through the category headings to find the right section. If you can't find the desired item, click inside the search box, type what you are looking for and click on the magnifying glass symbol to instigate a search that will bring up a list of what is available.

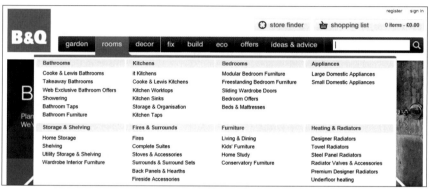

Reproduced with permission of @ B&Q 2012

Figure 17.1

After selecting Towel Radiators, we see a page similar to that shown in Figure 17.2. We now have 101 different items from which to choose. We can refine our search by brand or price and see what special offers may be available.

If you like the look of a particular item, click on it to display more details of the item. We have decided to purchase a suitable model as shown in Figure 17.3. Having read the specification and made our mind up, we check that the quantity box shows 1 and then click the Add to Shopping List button. This will now put the radiator in our shopping basket. Buying such a large item over the Internet may be strange, but this is one of the big plus points of being able to purchase nearly anything on line.

Don't worry — you have not committed yourself to the purchase yet. At this point, the company does not know your name, nevermind your address and credit card details.

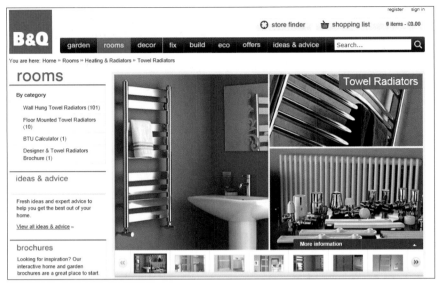

Reproduced with permission of @ B&Q 2012

Figure 17.2

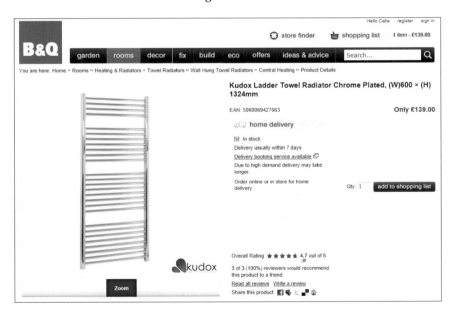

Reproduced with permission of @ B&Q 2012

Figure 17.3

Practice online shopping by dropping items into the shopping baskets of lots of different websites. There is no risk of making unwanted purchases. The more often you do this the faster your confidence will grow. You do not have to commit yourself to buying anything.

After you have finished adding items to your shopping basket, you will have the opportunity to view your basket or shopping list, Continue shopping or Checkout. When happy, click on the Checkout button. Figure 17.4 shows you the contents of our online shopping basket.

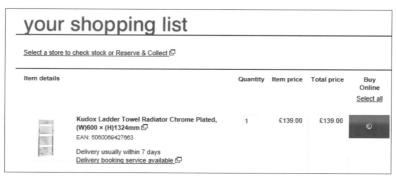

Reproduced with permission of @ B&Q 2012

Figure 17.4

Clicking on the Checkout button will take you to the next page where you are asked to sign in or continue without signing in. We will deal with registering with B&Q in just a moment, but for now look at the new web page and you will see at the top that the web address (URL) now starts with https://. This means that the page is secure and your details cannot be intercepted. There is also a padlock symbol on the right side of the address bar (see Figure 17.5). When both of these signs are present you can proceed, safe in the knowledge any details you submit will be encrypted to prevent illegal access to the information.

Padlock symbol

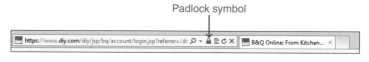

Figure 17.5

Registering with a website

With many companies, before you can buy anything you have to register your personal details, which will be held by the company and used for any future orders. In the case of B&Q you do not have to register, but this means you will have to enter your details to complete your order every time you buy something from the site. By registering, you can access your account very quickly in the future by entering your email address and password.

Completing your purchase

In this case, we choose to continue without registering so the next page asks you for personal information including name, address and telephone number. Carefully work your way through the various boxes. Note that all boxes marked with an asterisk are obligatory. If you fail to complete the form properly, you will be prompted to correct the mistakes.

It can become rather tedious placing the cursor in successive boxes using the mouse. There is a shortcut. Once you have completed one box, simply tap the Tab key and the cursor will jump to the next box. To reverse the action, use Shift + Tab.

Having filled in your personal details, click on Delivery Address and fill in the required details, as shown in Figure 17.6. In this case, there is a standard delivery charge of £5. Be careful here because some sites will automatically select a quicker, more expensive delivery option. If you are in no hurry, you can either get cheaper or even free delivery. Again, click on Continue.

Are you getting worried yet? Think about it. You have selected a purchase and typed in your email and home address but you have not entered your credit card details and nothing has been sent to the store yet.

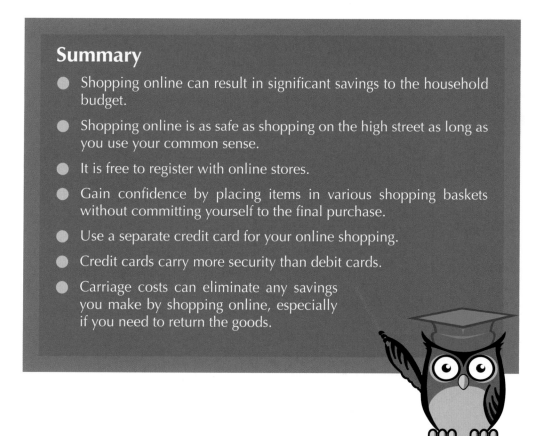

Reproduced with permission of @ B&Q 2012

Figure 17.6

Summary

- Shopping online can result in significant savings to the household budget.

- Shopping online is as safe as shopping on the high street as long as you use your common sense.

- It is free to register with online stores.

- Gain confidence by placing items in various shopping baskets without committing yourself to the final purchase.

- Use a separate credit card for your online shopping.

- Credit cards carry more security than debit cards.

- Carriage costs can eliminate any savings you make by shopping online, especially if you need to return the goods.

Brain training

There may be more than one correct answer to the following questions.

1. Why is online shopping cheaper than on the high street?

a) VAT is not charged on online purchases

b) Fewer staff are needed

c) Warehouses are cheaper than retail outlets

d) The Internet is cheaper than petrol and parking

2. How would you find the web address of a company?

a) From a catalogue or advertisement

b) By using a search engine

c) From an invoice

d) You simply have to guess

3. Why does a retail company need your email address?

a) To send confirmation of your order

b) For advertising purposes

c) To verify your identity

d) To send you unsolicited mail

4. Why do companies ask you to register with their site?

a) For retail analysis purposes

b) So that you do not have to enter your details every time you make a purchase from them

c) To keep you informed of their latest products on offer

d) For security reasons

5. When is it safe to provide your bank account details?

a) In the bank to a bona fide employee

b) By email

c) On an encrypted web page of a trusted company

d) To someone calling you on the telephone

Answers

Q1 – b, c and d   **Q2** – a, b and c   **Q3** – All four answers are correct

Q4 – a, b and c   **Q5** – a and c

Booking travel online

18

Equipment needed: Computer with screen, keyboard and mouse; Internet connection; ISP account; Windows 8 operating system; credit or debit card; printer.

Skills needed: Keyboard and mouse (Chapter 1), Windows 8 screens (Chapters 2 and 3), emailing (Chapter 12), knowledge of using the Internet browser (Chapter 13) and the ability to search the web (Chapter 16).

Travel, especially air travel, has become much cheaper in recent years, largely due to the increase in online booking. Airlines such as EasyJet, Ryanair and their competitors have been able to reduce air fares to ridiculous levels by insisting on web ticketing, forcing the big players like British Airways to follow suit. Central computerisation has also reduced the need for local travel agents to issue paper tickets, meaning the airlines pay them less commission. In these recessionary times, it can be difficult to stretch the budget to include family holidays but the battle for seat occupancy means that there are still opportunities for us, the travelling public, to travel economically. Having said that, cheap flight operators are now charging for so many 'extras' that real bargains are becoming harder to find.

There are hundreds of airlines offering good deals on the web. Check them out on the PCWisdom website (**www.pcwisdom.co.uk**) under the Price Comparison and Travel sections of the Internet Links page. Websites such as Kayak (**www.kayak. co.uk**) and Lastminute (**www.lastminute.com**) allow you to search for the best deals across the web.

Ticketless booking

This is where the airline emails you with a reference number or a ticket to print out yourself. You then present this at the check-in desk, where your details are available on the computer. It will feel very strange not to be clutching an old-fashioned ticket together with your passport and other documents as you approach the desk. The first time I used this system I definitely felt a frisson of anxiety but all went smoothly — it just takes a little getting used to.

Booking a flight with EasyJet

We are going to lead you gently through the process of booking a flight with the EasyJet airline. Let us imagine that you live in Manchester and fancy a short holiday in Cyprus. Use Google to confirm that the URL of EasyJet is **www.easyjet.com** and either click on the link or enter the web address in the address bar to access the airline's Home Page, which will look similar to Figure 18.1.

Reproduced by permission of easyJet airline company ltd

Figure 18.1

Companies are continually changing the appearance of their websites but the general principles outlined in this chapter will apply to all travel sites.

Most of the page is covered by current offers but you need to concentrate on the panel on the right. To the right of the Flying From box is a small downwards arrow. Click on this to raise the list of airports that EasyJet flies from. Scroll down and click on Manchester. Repeat the process with the arrow alongside the Going To box and choose Cyprus.

Now you have to check your diary to decide on a particular date — in this case Saturday 8, September 2012. Select this date by clicking on the Calendar icon to the right of the Outbound box. Repeat the process with the Return box. If you can be flexible about dates, tick the relevant box above the date entries and you will be shown any available options of slightly different dates offering cheaper prices. Finally click on Show Flights.

In Figure 18.2, you'll see that there are a number of flight options available for our chosen dates. We have chosen to fly in mid-season so the flights are moderately expensive — the columns on the right show the cheapest flight options through-out the year. We can still reduce the cost by opting to fly on the Sunday and return a week later, which would reduce the total cost of the tickets from £221.98 to £186.98, saving ourselves £35. (Make sure you know whether the cost is for a single or return ticket.) There is only one flight a day from Manchester to Cyprus but a London airport may offer more options with cheaper fares if you are pre-pared to fly at unsocial hours. You can also check out alternative dates by clicking on the three-week view. In our example, the return flight on Sunday does not arrive until 1:20 in the morning, so you might decide to check out other airports or airlines to avoid such a late arrival.

Reproduced by permission of easyJet airline company ltd

Figure 18.2

After you have chosen your flight, select it by clicking on it. Your Basket will be updated with your selection (see Figure 18.3). Click on Continue.

The next page offers additional options that you can add to your flight tickets, such as insurance, baggage charges, preferential boarding and any sports equipment such as golf bags. This is where your flight costs can begin to escalate. If we took up all the options in our example, we would add £90.73 to each individual ticket. If you don't need the additional options, don't add them. For example, can you travel with hand luggage only? Can you find cheaper travel insurance elsewhere? Will you be able to hire golf clubs for less than it would cost to take your own?

In this case (Figure 18.3) we have decided to take a bag each but we will be using our personal travel insurance. The next page reminds us that we have not opted for the airline's travel insurance, so we click on No Thanks and are taken to a page that offers options to book a hotel. We will be staying with friends so we do not need this and click on Continue.

Figure 18.3

As is the case when shopping online (see Chapter 17), you are still not committed to buying the flight at this stage.

The next page is where the serious business starts. The web address is now preceded by https:// denoting that it is a secure page and, to confirm this, the padlock symbol appears. Enter your email address so EasyJet knows how to contact you and, since you have not booked with the airline before, you will have to enter your personal details. Click on I'm New to easyjet.com and Continue. Confirm your email address, then enter your address and telephone number, together with details of your accompanying passengers, before completing the payment details. You can complete this form quite safely without committing yourself to the purchase — just *don't* click on Book Now until you are prepared to commit to the transaction. Before going ahead with the booking, tick the box agreeing to the airline's terms and conditions.

And that's it!

This example did not take long because we had already decided on a destination, home airport and date. In reality, you might spend a while exploring the various ways of getting to Cyprus using different airlines, different airports, different dates and times — and finding out whether you would get a better deal by taking your holiday in Crete!

Low-fare advertisements

You have probably seen 'unbelievable' offers of flights for £1.99 in national newspapers. These offers are often for flights at unsocial times or limited to a few tickets for unsold seats the airline needs to fill. You will still have to pay for 'extras' such as baggage, and the return flight may be considerably more expensive. Having said that, you will often find much cheaper flights if you book well in advance or make a late booking (although you risk the flight being fully booked), or opt for a flight at an unsocial hour.

Booking train and coach travel

Coach and rail tickets are also much cheaper if booked online. One popular UK website for rail tickets is Trainline (**www.thetrainline.com**). Another one for the UK is **www.nationalrail.co.uk**, which is very useful for journey planning. In the US, Amtrak is the main website (**www.amtrak.com**) while European train tickets can be purchased from Rail Europe (**www.raileurope.co.uk**) or Rail Travel Europe (**www.eurail.com**). Rail companies have their own websites, which may offer better prices. Use Google to search for your local rail franchise such as First Capital Connect, East Midlands Trains and First Great Western Trains.

To give you more practice in booking travel tickets, we are going to book a return rail journey from Bristol to Edinburgh.

Type Trainline's address (**www.thetrainline.com**) into the address bar, hit the Return key and you will be presented with the company's home page (see Figure 18.4). As you will see, the site not only offers UK train tickets but also Eurostar tickets, hotels, car hire and theatre tickets.

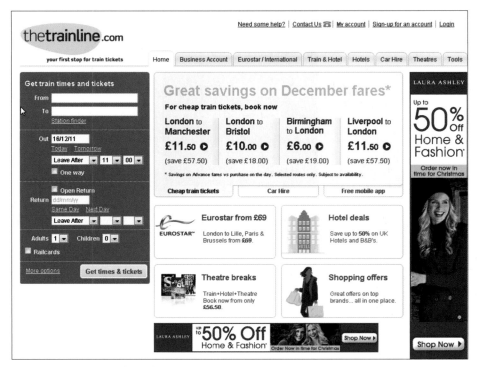

Reproduced by permission of thetrainline.com

Figure 18.4

Move the cursor to the From box (see Figure 18.5) and type in your station of departure — in our case, Bristol. A dropdown menu then offers a selection of stations that fit your description so click on the correct one. Repeat the process in the To box for your destination. Click on the Out box and a calendar appears allowing you to select your departure date. Do the same for the Return date. Choose a time option, bearing in mind that booking a ticket outside busy commuting hours will reduce the price of the journey.

If you hold a railcard, tick the Railcard box and a further selection menu will appear allowing you to register your card. Finally click on Get Times & Tickets to see the range of options and the number of changes involved in the journey.

Click on the Show Prices option and the full details will be displayed, as in Figure 18.6.

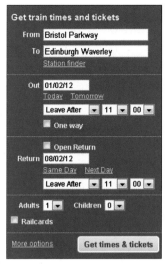

Reproduced by permission of thetrainline.com

Figure 18.5

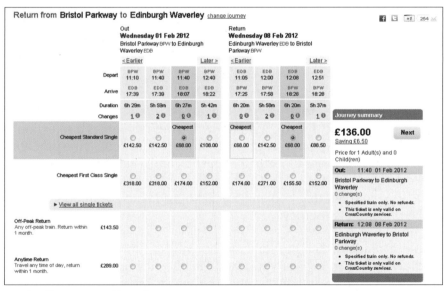

Reproduced by permission of thetrainline.com

Figure 18.6

Select the ticket you want by clicking on the round radio button below the journey option and a journey summary will appear in the right column. Click on the Next button to display the travel options, such as which way you prefer to face, the seat position and coach type. Tick any other preferences before clicking Continue to take you to the next page, where you will enter your email address and then select Sign Up.

This is the first 'secure' page to appear because you are being asked for personal information. The page address now starts with 'https://' and the padlock symbol is shown, so you can be sure that any such information will be encrypted.

Complete the necessary personal details and choose a suitable password to register and continue to the next page. This gives you the options of printing your own tickets, having the tickets posted to you or collecting your tickets from a self-service ticket dispenser at the station. If you choose the latter, you will need to take the credit card you used to make the payment together with a reference number you are given.

At this point, you are still perfectly safe to continue with this practice exercise without committing yourself to buying the ticket. The next page summarises your journey costs. Check that these are correct and tick the box confirming that you accept the terms and conditions before proceeding to the final payment page. If you are following this as a practice exercise, here is where you stop. To complete an actual purchase, enter your credit card details and activate the Buy Tickets option. Depending on the ticketing option you have chosen, you will be given a reference number, instructions about printing your tickets or simple confirmation of your purchase. This will be confirmed by an email that should be sent to you within 30 minutes of your purchase.

These two examples should give you enough confidence to start practising. Take your time over each page and practice clicking on the various options to gain confidence — you do not have to commit yourself to a purchase. Play around with various booking sites. They all vary slightly but the general principles remain the same. If at any stage you omit an essential step, you will be returned to the page in question automatically, with the missing details highlighted.

Summary

- Booking travel online can result in significant savings.

- Practice 'booking' imaginary journeys to gain experience and confidence.

- Travelling at less social hours and on certain days of the week will reduce the costs.

- The cheapest seats will sell out quickly so try to book well in advance of your holiday.

- Extra baggage will significantly increase the ticket price and, with some airlines, it is cheaper if you take hand luggage only.

- Third party annual travel insurance policies are a lot cheaper than single journey insurance offered by the travel company.

- Avoid busy commuting times to get better prices.

- Online travel booking is not restricted to the UK. European and US travel can be booked just as easily.

Brain training

There may be more than one correct answer to the following questions.

1. Where have all the cheap advertised flights gone?

   a) They were snapped up very quickly

   b) They only apply to night flights

   c) You must fly from a regional airport to get them

   d) There were very few of them

2. What happens if you press the Submit button twice?

   a) You will get a rude email from the airline company

   b) You will order two flights

   c) Nothing. The computer will recognise the mistake and ignore it

   d) The whole booking will be cancelled

3. Which of the following options may reduce the cost of your flight?

   a) Flying at the last minute

   b) Booking well in advance

   c) Booking by telephone

   d) Flying at unsocial times

4. Which of the following might cover you if you have to cancel a flight because of illness?

   a) A debit card

   b) Holiday insurance

   c) A credit card

   d) Your household policy

Answers

Q1 – a and d

Q3 – b and d

Q2 – b

Q4 – b and c

Entertainment

19

Equipment needed: A computer with screen, keyboard and mouse; an Internet connection; an ISP account; Windows 8 operating system; a credit or debit card and a printer.

Skills needed: Keyboard and mouse (Chapter 1), Windows 8 screens (Chapters 2 and 3), emailing (Chapter 12), knowledge of using the Internet browser (Chapter 13) and the ability to search the web (Chapter 16).

After they get their computer set up, many members of the older generation seem content to stick with the basics of email and searching the Internet with the occasional foray into buying goods or services. However, a whole world of entertainment and hobbies is waiting to be explored. You can have music playing in the background while you compose an email or put the finishing touches to the minutes of the fixtures committee of your local tennis club.

Playing CDs and DVDs

You may have CDs of your favourite music lying on a bookshelf. Why not have some soothing music playing while you try and sort out a computing problem? Simply open the CD tray, insert the disc and choose your favourite tracks. As soon as a CD is placed in the tray and closed, a small message may appear in the top-right corner of the screen asking you what you want to do with the CD. Click or tap on the message to play the CD. This will open a small window in the top-left corner of the screen (Figure 19.1) while the music begins to play. Using the window controls you can pause the track, alter the volume or return to the list of the recorded tracks.

Tapping or clicking on the Library icon opens the Windows Media Player window in Desktop mode showing the contents of the CD you are playing, as shown in Figure 19.2. By tapping or clicking on the various tracks, you can pick different songs or simply allow the computer to play the tracks in order. You can pause the playing by using the Play/Pause button and resume listening when it suits you.

Playing your CDs this way is fine if you are happy to keep changing the CDs as your listening interests change, but you will open up a whole new world of personal music if you transfer the contents of the CD to the computer. This process is known as *ripping* a CD.

Figure 19.1

Folders   Create playlist   Rip CD   CD contents   Burn CD

Figure 19.2

Ripping music

Ripping a CD does not mean causing irreparable damage to the CD but rather copying music tracks from the disc to the computer. If the contents of your music library are stored on the computer, you don't need to change the CD every time you want to listen to a different artist.

Simply tapping or clicking on the Rip CD icon initiates the copying process and continues until the whole disc has been copied to the Music library of the computer. You may want to copy only certain tracks from the CD in which case deselect the check box alongside the tracks that you want to omit.

Creating playlists

After you have accumulated a number of musical numbers in the Music library, you can create individual playlists that reflect your current mood. Click or tap on the Create Playlist icon. A new playlist folder will appear waiting to be given a descriptive title. Once you have created the playlist title, you only have to open up the library and drag the tracks onto the playlist folder to create your own personal selection.

Creating a personal CD

After you've created a personal playlist, you can copy your favourite music to a CD to use in your car or other CD player. Place a blank CD in the CD tray, select the playlist folder and click on the Burn tab. *Burning* is the technical term for copying computer contents to a CD. The computer will automatically copy the tracks to the disc, which you can then use away from the computer.

Playing DVDs

Unfortunately, Windows 8 has removed the DVD function from its Media Player. You will have to download the Media Center from the App store. Once installed, it is a simple matter of inserting the DVD and tapping or clicking on the options.

Windows 8 Music app

The Windows 8 Music app offers a different view of your music collection using the Start screen. Tap or click on the Music tile on the Start menu.

Tap or click on the album you wish to hear and the music will strike up immediately. To view the menu options, right-click or swipe up from the bottom of the screen. Now you can use the Play/Pause button in the same way you used it when watching videos (see Figure 19.3).

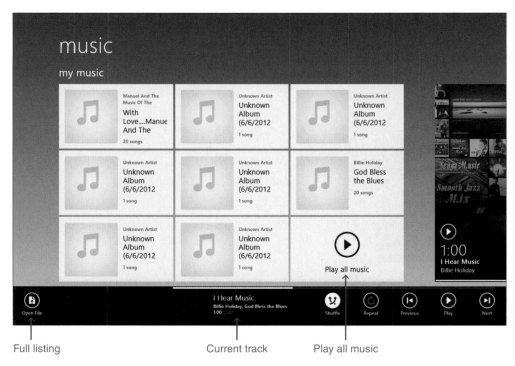

Full listing   Current track   Play all music

Figure 19.3

Clicking on the Shuffle button will play your tracks in random order. To view the list of tracks on a particular album, tap or click on the album tile (see Figure 19.4).

This app screen allows you to select individual tracks using the left-click while the right-click menu offers the options of shuffling and repeating the selected tracks.

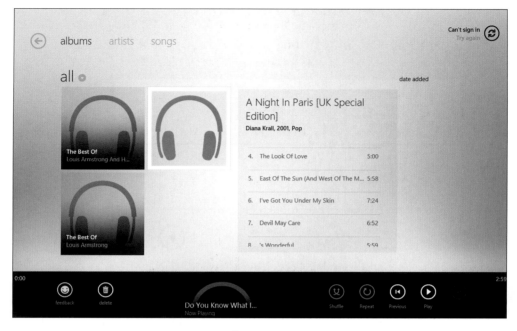

Figure 19.4

Spotify

There may be occasions when you fancy a particular piece of music that you do not have on a CD or that you may want to download from the Internet. Spotify will satisfy both of these needs. There are literally millions of music tracks available for listening and, if you are prepared to accept advertisements on the screen, they are all free. Almost every artist is featured from Dame Nellie Melba and Enrico Caruso to JLS.

To download the program you must first register with Spotify, which is free. You can do this through any Facebook account you may have created or directly with Spotify. Spotify can be downloaded from **www.spotify.com** where you will find that there are three subscription rates:

● The first is free but you have to accept the advertisements.

● The Unlimited subscription costs £4.99 a month but eliminates the adverts.

● The final account is called a Premium account which dispenses with the advertisements and allows you to create off line playlists and unlimited downloading of the music tracks for a cost of £9.99 a month.

After you are registered, you will be presented with the download page shown in Figure 19.5. Click on Get Spotify and then tap or click the Run option at the bottom of the screen. The download follows roughly the same process described in Chapter 15.

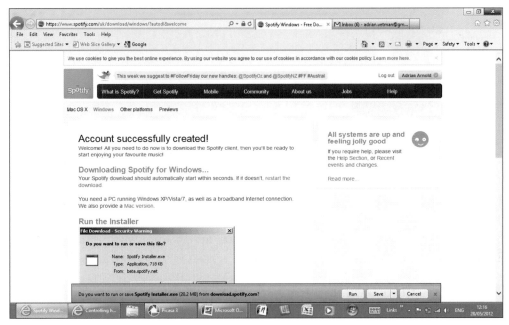

The Spotify logo is the registered trademark of the Spotify group of companies and screenshots are (c) Spotify Ltd 2012. All rights reserved.

Figure 19.5

Figure 19.6 shows a typical window playing a particular track together with artwork of the album. Use the Search box to find artists and songs. You will be offered a selection of tracks, artists and albums. Click or tap on the desired collection and then tap or click on the selected track to play it. By minimizing the window, you can have your favourite music playing in the background while you get on with other work.

Search box

Playlists

Playing
track

Figure 19.6

Listening to the radio on the computer

Many websites offer radio broadcasts from across the world including the following:

- **www.bbc.co.uk/radio** broadcasts UK radio stations.

- **http://www.live-radio.net/worldwide.shtml** offers thousands of radio programs from around the world from Armenia to the Yemen.

- **www.tunein.com** offers local radio, music and sports commentary from across the globe.

Many people from abroad like to keep in touch with their home country; others use foreign radio stations to brush up their language skills.

TV players

Many TV channels offer opportunities to catch up on broadcasts that you may have missed. They are free to use — provided you have a television licence — but many programs are only available for a certain period of time. Many people will be aware of the BBC iPlayer but ignorant of the fact that many other channels offer the catch-up experience, some of which are listed next:

You will need a reasonably fast Internet connection of about 2 Meg to avoid irritating interruptions while the computer catches up with the downloading process.

- The BBC iPlayer found at **www.bbc.co.uk/iplayer** makes most programs available for 7 days after the original transmission. The iPlayer also stores recent radio programs if you have missed a particular broadcast.

- The ITV player at **www.itv.com/itvplayer** retains programs for 30 days.

- Channel 4 uses 4 Catch Up at **www.channel4.com/watch_online**. (Note that the character between 'watch' and 'online' is an underscore character (_) and not the hyphen (-).) These programs are also held for 30 days post-transmission.

- Demand Five at **www.channel5.com/demand5** holds programs for 30 days.

The best way to learn how to use these recording programs is to play around with them. Experiment! You will not incur any charges and you can always close the web page down if you get into a mess.

Movies on the computer

There are a number of companies offering films and TV programs on subscription terms. Netflix at **www.netflix.com** allows unlimited viewing of thousands of films for a monthly subscription of £5.99. LoveFilm at **www.lovefilm.com** charges £4.99 per month for unlimited access to more than 5,000 films and TV episodes. One advantage of the subscription services is that you avoid interruption by adverts.

All TV players and movie downloads are displayed in a similar way to that used by other video services such as YouTube as explained in Chapter 16. By right-clicking or swiping from the bottom of the screen, you will be able to play, pause and rewind the broadcast.

Slide shows

In Chapter 15, we suggested that you try to download the Picasa program. If you managed to achieve this, the Picasa tile will be available at the right end of the Start menu. Tap or click on the tile to initiate the program. The first time the program is run it will catalogue all the pictures stored on the computer and collate them into folders, as shown in Figure 19.7. Tap or click on a folder to reveal its contents, and then tap or click on the Green Slide Show arrow to play a continuous slide show of your holiday snaps.

Figure 19.7

Picasa is much more than a cataloguing system. There are many basic fixes available to improve your images. By double-clicking on a particular image it will appear in the Editing window (see Figure 19.8).

Figure 19.8

We suggest experimenting with the various options available. Any editing function is reversible so you will not corrupt your photos by testing out the various editing tools. If you want to retain a permanent record of your improved photo, then you can use the Save As command in the File menu and give it a different name. In this way, you retain both the original and corrected images.

There is not room in a book of this kind to explore the full capabilities of the Picasa program, but we can recommend a companion volume in the *Older and Wiser* series — *Digital Photography for the Older and Wiser* by Kim Gilmour.

If you wish to explore further use of the Internet we would refer you to *The Internet for the Older and Wiser* by Adrian Arnold.

Summary

- The computer can do so much more than send emails and search the Internet.

- CDs can be played directly from the CD tray or loaded onto the computer for future listening.

- Music can be downloaded from the Internet for a small fee and stored on the computer.

- Listen to the radio on your computer while working on other projects.

- Catch up on your favourite TV programs by using the various TV players.

- Subscribing to various film sites allows you to watch your favourite movies.

- Have friends round for supper and play a slide show of your recent holiday while you finish the cooking.

- Improve your digital photos by using Picasa. Any editing you do is completely reversible.

Brain training

There may be more than one correct answer to these questions.

1. How can you play music on the computer?

   a) Place a CD into the computer tray

   b) You need a licence

   c) Tap on the Music app tile

   d) Open Windows Media Player to access music stored on the computer

2. How can you play a recent TV broadcast?

   a) You will need a broadband connection

   b) You will need a satellite dish

   c) You will need a Wi-Fi connection

   d) The computer needs to be connected to the TV

3. How would you play a slide show of your photographs?

   a) Use a slide projector

   b) Use Picasa

   c) Use the Windows Media Player

   d) Use the Pictures library

4. What do you need to play a movie on the computer?

   a) A DVD player program

   b) A broadband connection of at least 2 Meg

   c) A very large hard disc

   d) A subscription to YouTube

Answers

Q1 – a, c and d

Q2 – a and c if you want to use a laptop without a cable connection to the router

Q3 – b, c and d

Q4 – a and b

Introducing social networking

Equipment needed: A computer with screen, keyboard and mouse; an Internet connection; an ISP account; Windows 8 operating system; a credit or debit card and a printer.

Skills needed: Keyboard and mouse (Chapter 1), Windows 8 screens (Chapters 2 and 3), emailing (Chapter 12), knowledge of using the Internet browser (Chapter 13) and the ability to search the web (Chapter 16).

Social networking seems to be the buzz phrase of the moment, but what is it? It is simply a way of making and retaining contact with people often with similar interests or backgrounds. Even those people who have no interest in computing will have heard of Twitter and Facebook. They are only two of hundreds of social networking sites available on the Internet. Apart from the well-known sites, there are networking sites for almost every interest. There are sites that put you back in contact with old school friends and work colleagues. Other sites allow you to build up contacts related to your trade or profession, your ethnic background, hobbies and interests. You can post your opinions on photographs, politics, films and books and even find a partner for life.

In this book, we can only touch the surface of the range of such sites. To view a list of most of the social networking sites you go to Wikipedia at **www.wikipedia.org** and search for social networking sites. We recommend *Social Networking for the Older and Wiser* by Sean McManus if you want to explore your social networking options further.

Using Facebook

This site has more than 900 million members. Like most of these sites, registration is free. Go to **www.facebook.com** to open the registration page.

 It is possible to delete a Facebook account but it can prove to be a complicated procedure so read about it before you commit yourself to signing up.

Fill in the boxes and tap or click on Sign Up. After you create your account, which only takes a couple of minutes, you will need to add a few friends. If you have a Contact list on a Gmail or Hotmail account, Facebook will scroll through the list and display those contacts who have a Facebook account. You can then choose to add them to your list of Facebook friends. The next tab will ask you to enter the name of your school, college, university and employer. This information is not obligatory but provides useful information to your correspondents. Finally, you can add a profile picture from an image stored on the computer or taken by a webcam on your laptop.

Privacy settings allow you to restrict access to certain people. Unless you stipulate who can view your details, everything you put on your Facebook page is available to the public. You must select the groups of contacts who can view this information. The privacy settings are accessed by editing your profile.

After you have identified those friends you wish to add to your list, a message will be sent to each individual asking them if they are prepared to accept you as a friend. Only when they have accepted your invitation will their details appear on your list of friends.

After the account is set up, you can begin to post comments on what is happening in your life or upload photographs. You can also send messages to specific friends.

Facebook even reminds you of your friends' birthdays and other anniversaries!

Pick your friends carefully. Don't just add people for the sake of increasing the size of your list. Your personal details are available to all and sundry, so be careful with any information you provide. There is a particularly unpleasant practice called 'trolling' when people post bullying and vilifying messages for all to see. Employers are making increasing use of social networking sites when considering an offer of employment.

You can edit your profile details at any time so, after you feel safe about your personal information, you can start to post a few messages, play some online games or publish photos of your latest holiday.

Twitter

This networking site has 300 million subscribers. It is designed for short messages of no more than 140 characters. You can sign up to use Twitter at **www.twitter. com**. This site finds more favour with the younger members of society who want to keep up with the daily lives of pop stars and Premier League footballers. Not everything on Twitter is about Wayne Rooney shopping at Tesco. Modern communications mean that news is constantly evolving and many businesses need to keep abreast of current developments. Twitter messages, known as *tweets*, can alert people to developing situations before it hits the news agencies. For example, a financial institution may get advance information about a particular business story by following the tweets of a reputable financial correspondent before he releases the story on the 6 o'clock news.

LinkedIn

Found at **www.linkedin.com**, this is an invaluable site for business networking across the globe. It provides lists of potential professional advisors on every subject under the sun.

Friends Reunited

This site has been operating since July 2000 and now boasts 19 million subscribers. It started as a way of reuniting school friends but has developed to include workplace colleagues, events, places and childhood memories. Register at **www. friendsreunited.com**, and you will be taken on a tour of the facilities offered by the site.

Many lapsed friendships have been revived by the use of this site. You can search for people by educational establishment, work, service career and many other criteria.

If you are interested in researching your family history, there is a very useful companion site to Friends Reunited called Genes Reunited at **www.genesreunited. co.uk**. Another respected genealogy site is Ancestry.co.uk. These sites offer access to every census from 1841 to 1911 but also inform you of likely family matches in other members' family trees. There are more than 515 million historical records available on these sites. Registration is free, but you will have to pay to view the detailed census pages. Once again, there is a very useful book in the series to aid your genealogy research — *Family History for the Older and Wiser* by Sue Fifer.

Summary

● There are hundreds of social networking sites available on the net.

● In most cases registration is free as the site operators gain their revenue from advertising.

● Take care when filling in your personal details and posting messages. The information can be accessed by almost anyone unless you have established strong privacy settings.

● Twitter confines messages to 140 characters but you can send multiple messages on the same subject.

● Old school friends, military service companions and work colleagues can be contacted using Friends Reunited.

● Research your family tree with Genes Reunited or Ancestry.co.uk

● Get detailed information on social networking sites by reading *Social Networking for the Older and Wiser.*

Brain training

There may be more than one correct answer to these questions.

1. What is a social networking site?

a) A website that requires an invitation

b) A group of people with similar interests

c) A website that arranges reunions

d) A group of people with left wing politics

2. Who can view your details on Facebook if you have not set the Privacy settings?

a) Only those registered as family

b) Only those on your list of friends

c) Anybody

d) Those people who have received specific permission from you

3. How many characters can you use in a tweet?

a) 120

b) 150

c) 140

d) 200

4. Which of the following are social networking sites?

a) Facebook

b) Twitter

c) Gogoyoko

d) AsianAvenue

Answers

Q1 – b

Q3 – c

Q2 – c

Q4 – all of them

Glossary

ADSL Asymmetric Digital Subscriber Line. Broadband Internet connection that is 300 – 200 times faster and allows permanent connection. To receive this, you need to be close to a digital telephone exchange, on cable or have a satellite dish.

adware Advertising software that causes adverts to appear on your screen, either by invitation or (more likely) without your permission.

antivirus program A program that can spot and deal with a virus attached to an email or already on your computer.

application or app A program that performs a specific task. *See* Program.

backup Copies of programs or work kept in a separate place in case something happens to the original version.

bandwidth A measure of the maximum amount of data that can be transferred over the Internet or phone system at any one time.

Bing Microsoft's Internet search engine.

bit The smallest unit of computer data. There are 8 bits to a byte. A character, number or space, usually takes up one byte. *See also* byte, gigabyte, kilobyte, megabyte.

blog, blogger A weblog. A diary, which can be on any subject, posted on the web. People who write blogs are known as bloggers.

boot To turn on a PC.

broadband High-bandwidth Internet connections such as Cable or ADSL, used for faster connections.

browser Program for browsing the Internet (eg Internet Explorer, Google Chrome or Mozilla Firefox).

byte A unit of computer data. There are 8 bits to a byte. A character, number or space, usually takes up one byte on a hard, floppy disk or CD. *See also* bit, gigabyte, kilobyte, megabyte.

CD/CD-ROM/CD-R/CDRW Compact Disk Read-Only Memory. The familiar disk on which programs arrive. They are read-only because the tracks are burnt onto them and cannot be changed. The RW type can be rewritten over many times.

chip The silicon base used to mount the millions of components that make up a computer processor.

clipart A ready-made picture on disk.

cloud computing A means for you to store and access your data/programs on the Internet instead of (or as well as) storing them on your own PC.

control panel An important set of icons that allow you to configure the basic functions of your computer.

cookie A small text file that is downloaded to your computer without your knowledge. They are often used to track your activities for marketing purposes.

download The process of transferring files from the web to your machine's hard drive. You can download pictures, text and programs.

drag and drop The facility in most programs to select text or a file and drag it to another position.

driver Software that enables certain peripherals to work, such as printers, sound cards and cameras.

dropdown menu The sub menu that is revealed when you click an item on a main menu.

DVD-ROM Digital Versatile Disk Read-Only Memory. A disk capable of containing much more than a CD. Used for music, films and *big* programs.

DVD-RW A rewriteable DVD.

email Messages sent to people over the Internet. Email addresses always contain the @ symbol.

Favorites Also known as bookmarks. All web browsers allow you to add your favorite websites to a list for easy retrieval.

firewall A program that ensures that your PC cannot be accessed by hackers.

gigabyte (GB) A thousand million bytes. *See also* bit, byte, kilobyte, megabyte.

hard disk A set of spinning disks coated with recording material. Can retain details of programs and data indefinitely.

hardware Any piece of equipment, such as the computer or a printer.

Home Page The first (main) page of a website.

icon A graphic representation of something such as a shortcut to a program or an action within a program.

interface An initial screen on the screen that provides access to different apps and programs.

Internet A vast network of linked computers that can be accessed by people who are connected to the web.

Java and JavaScript A programming language used on some web pages.

JPG or JPEG Joint Photographic Expert Group. The most commonly used compressed graphic format for picture files.

kilobyte (KB) A thousand bytes. *See also* bit, byte, gigabyte, megabyte.

malware Software that arrives on your computer that is damaging or malicious, such as viruses or spyware.

megabyte A million bytes. *See also* bit, byte, gigabyte, kilobyte.

MP3 A highly compressed form of music, which can be downloaded from the Net and played on a computer or portable MP3 player.

MSN Microsoft Network.

online Connected to the Internet.

pixel Picture element. A small element on a screen or in a photograph. A megapixel is a million pixels. The more pixels the better the quality of the picture and the more memory is used.

program A system that allows the computer to achieve specific ends, such as word processing or managing financial accounts. *See* software.

router A gadget that connects one or more computers to the Internet.

search engine A program, usually accessed on the Net, that enables you to search for what you want by entering a few words.

software Programs of all kinds that make the computer act in a particular way.

spam Unsolicited advertising that usually arrives as an email.

spyware Software maliciously installed on your computer without your knowledge to monitor and report back what you are doing.

toolbar A list of icons often found at the top of programs such as word processors.

Trojan A virus program that is disguised as something else. It invades your PC and can be accessed by a hacker.

USB port Universal Serial Bus port. A socket, about half an inch long, that allows you to connect other devices to your computer and data to be transferred between them.

virus A malicious program that can harm your computer. It is spread through other programs, either from disks or from the Internet. They may also be called Trojans or worms.

webcam A small camera attached to a computer.

Wi-Fi A wireless interface that uses radio to link a computer to other devices.

worm A virus program that spreads by sending itself to people in an infected computer's email address book.

WWW World Wide Web. The Internet.

Index

Symbols

&123 key on virtual keyboard, 33

A

action centre, system tray icon, 55
activating new software, 228
address bar, web browser, 192, 241
address book (contacts), 182, 213–217
Adobe Flash Player, 244
ADSL (Asymmetric Digital Subscriber
        Line), defined, 293
adware, defined, 293
Aero Peek, 60
air travel booking online, 261–266
Alt key, 31
antivirus program, 157–158, 293
Apple iPad, 9, 24
applications (Desktop). *See also*
        WordPad
  apps, compared to, 21–22
  Backspace key, 29, 117, 124–125
  defined, 293

  Delete key, 124–125
  deleting text, 122, 124–125
  dropdown menus, 120–121
  finding files, 128
  formatting text, 118–119
  inserting text, 122
  installing, 223–233
  Internet Explorer, 78–79, 190–196
  opening an application, 115–117
  Quick Access bar, 122–123
  ribbon, 66–67
  saving a text document, 125–128
  selecting text, 117–118, 121–122
  Undo and Redo icons, 124
  uninstalling, 40
Arnold, Adrian (author)
  *The Internet for the
    Older and Wiser,* 283
arrow navigation keys, 125
Ask search engine, 247
Asymmetric Digital Subscriber Line
        (ADSL), defined, 293
&123 key on virtual keyboard, 33
attachments to email, 156, 179–180
audio, listening to, 276–278

B

background, Desktop, 58
backing up your data/files,
162–165, 293
Backspace key, 29, 117, 124–125
bandwidth, defined, 293
battery level and Wi-Fi status, system
tray icon, 55
battery usage settings, 96
Bing search engine, 111, 247, 293
bit, defined, 149, 293
blog or blogger, defined, 293
booking online travel, 261–269
boot, defined, 293
breadcrumb bar, 67
broadband Internet connection,
147–148, 294
browser, web
defined, 294
Internet Explorer app, 196–199
Internet Explorer application
(Desktop), 78–79, 190–196
introduction, 189–190
bundling communication services,
defined, 148
burning (copying) files to CD, 276
byte, defined, 149, 294

C

Caps Lock key, 30
CD
burning music files to, 276
defined, 294
installing an application from,
223–228
playing music from, 273
ripping music tracks from, 274–275

Change PC Settings, 89
Charms menu, 34, 43–47
Checkout button at web stores, 256
chip, silicon computer, defined, 294
clicking action with mouse, 24–25
clipart, defined, 294
Close button, Desktop window, 65
cloud computing, 164, 294
coach tickets, booking online, 266
colours, changing text, 121
commercial software type, 229
computer equipment (hardware), 8–12
Computer section of window
side bar, 68
contacts, 182, 213–217
context-sensitive menu, 25
Control Panel, 95, 294
cookie, website, defined, 294
copying music to or from CD, 274–276
copyright issues for program software,
226, 228–230
credit cards, shopping on Internet, 161
Ctrl key, 30–31
currency conversion, 242
cursor in text document, 116, 117

D

data, defined, 76
date and time, system tray icon, 55–56
definitions of words, searching for, 242
Delete key, 29, 33, 117, 124–125
Deleted items folder, email, 176
deleting
all data from hard disk (Reset), 93
email messages, 181
folders, 80
text, 122, 124–125
desktop computer type, 9, 27

Desktop interface. *See also* documents
  applications compared to apps, 21–22
  background, changing, 58
  Backspace key, 29, 117, 124–125
  Delete key, 124–125
  dropdown menus, 120–121
  email in, 182–185
  finding files, 128
  getting started, 20–21
  icons, 53
  installing applications, 223–233
  Internet Explorer, 78–79, 190–196
  introduction, 51–53
  opening an application, 115–117
  organising, 56–60
  Quick Access bar, 122–123
  Recycle bin, 53–54
  ribbon, 66–67
  searching from, 96–97
  showing the Desktop, 60
  system tray icons, 54–56
  taskbar, 54
  Undo and Redo icons, 124
  uninstalling applications, 40
  windows, elements of, 63–70
Devices in Charms menu, 45
dialup Internet connection, defined,
        147, 148
*Digital Photography for the Older and
        Wiser* (Gilmour), 283
directions to a location (Maps), 110–111
disc, installing applications from,
        223–228. *See also* CD
disks and disk space, 76, 77, 78, 93,
        163–164, 295
documents, working in
  deleting text, 122, 124–125
  dropdown menus, 120–121
  finding files, 128
  fonts, changing, 118–119, 120
  formatting text, 118–119

  inserting text, 122
  Microsoft Word, compared to, 224
  opening, 115–117
  Quick Access bar, 122–123
  saving, 125–128
  selecting text, 117–118, 121–122
  Undo and Redo icons, 124
double-clicking with mouse, 25
downloading
  defined, 294
  limits from ISPs, 149
  music from Spotify, 278–280
  programs from Internet, 209–210,
        230–233
Drafts folder, email, 175
drag and drop technique with mouse,
        25, 81, 294
drive, defined, 76
driver software, defined, 294
Dropbox, 165
dropdown menu, 120–121, 294
DVD, playing movie from, 276, 294

E

EasyJet flight booking exercise, 262–266
economics of web-based commerce,
        251–252
email
  account setup, 172–173
  attachments to messages, 156,
        179–180
  contacts, relationship to, 182
  defined, 4–5, 295
  deleting messages, 181
  Desktop interface, 182–185
  email addresses, 172–173, 176
  folders, 174–176
  forwarding messages, 181
  Internet's role in providing, 144–145

email *(continued)*
    introduction, 171–172
    junk or spam email, 176, 180–181
    Mail app, 173–181
    opening, 173–174
    receiving and reading messages,
        179–180, 185
    replying to messages, 181
    sending messages, 176–178, 184–185
    spam or junk email, 176, 180–181
    web-based accounts, 182
Emoticon key on virtual keyboard, 33
encryption of information in online
        transactions, 160–161
Enter key, 28
Esc key, 29–30
external disk, 76, 163–164

F

F1 key for accessing Help, 132
Facebook, 288–289
family history, social networking
        resource for, 290
Family History for the Older and Wiser
        (Fifer), 290
Favorites menu, Internet Explorer,
        194–195, 295
Fifer, Sue (author)
    *Family History for the Older and
        Wiser,* 290
file attachments to email, 156, 179–180
File tab on ribbon, 66
filenames, inserting, 125
files. *See also* documents
    backing up, 162–165, 293
    copying, 83, 274–276
    disks and disk space, 76, 77, 78
    drives, 76
    external storage for, 76, 163–164

introduction, 75
Libraries, 77, 78–79
memory, 76
moving, 81–82
renaming, 83
saving, 80, 83–85, 163–164
searching for, 128
selecting multiple, 82
Fill tool in Paint app, 107
financial transactions, protecting,
        8, 159–162, 252–253
finding files, 128. *See also* searching
firewall, 167, 295
Flash Player, 244
flicking gesture on touchscreen, 23
Flight mode for wireless connection,
        45–46, 94
Fn key, 31
folders
    creating new, 78–80, 126–127
    deleting, 80
    Mail app, 174–176
    renaming, 79
    viewing options, 66
font formatting, 118–119, 120
formatting text, 118–119, 120
forwarding email messages, 181
free space on hard drive, checking, 77
freeware software type, 229
Friends Reunited, 290
function keys, 31

G

gadgets on Desktop, 56
genealogy, online resources for, 290
gigabyte (GB), defined, 295
Gilmour, Kim (author)
    *Digital Photography for the
        Older and Wiser,* 283

Google
 changing Home Page to, 195–196
 online data storage service, 164
 search engine, 238–247
 web-based email, 182
Google Earth, 229

H

hard disk, 76, 77, 78, 93, 163–164, 295
hardware, computer, 8–12, 295
Help function, 67, 131–138
Hibernation mode, 96
hoaxes, online, 158
Home button, Internet Explorer, 192
Home Page, Internet Explorer, 191,
 195–196, 295
Home toolbar ribbon, 79
HomeGroup, shared network, 68, 94
Hotmail, 173
hovering for pop-up information,
 67, 118
hung program problem, 135–137

I

icon, defined, 53, 295
identity theft, 8, 156
image search, 242–243
Inbox, email, 174–175
insertion point, defined, 116, 117
installing applications
 copyright issues, 228–230
 from disc, 223–228
 from Internet, 230–233
interface, defined, 295
internal disk, defined, 76
Internet. *See also* email; security
 broadband connection, 147–148, 294
 costs of, 148–149

 defined, 4–6, 295
 dialup connection, 147, 148
 entertainment, 273–283
 equipment considerations, 10
 Help facility's connection to, 132
 as information resource, 3, 5, 135
 installing programs from, 209–210,
  230–233
 ISP, 143–144, 145–147, 172
 password, 150–151
 paying for, 151
 physical connections, 10
Internet
 schematic of workings, 144
 search engines, 111, 238–247, 253
 setting up, 149
 sharing access to, 68, 94, 166–167
 shopping on, 11, 159–162, 251–258
 social networking, 214, 287–290
 speed of connection, 147–148
 storage for files on, 164–165
 travel, booking online, 261–269
 username, 150
 wireless connection, 10, 45–46, 94,
  146, 165–167, 296
 World Wide Web, compared to,
  144, 189–190
Internet Explorer app, 196–199
Internet Explorer application (Desktop)
 address bar, 192
 Favorites menu, 194–195
 Home button, 192
 Home Page, 191, 195–196
 links, 193
 menu bar, 193–194
 navigation buttons, 192
 scrollbar, 195
 tabs bar, 193
 Windows Explorer, compared
  to, 78–79
Internet radio, 280

iPad for the Older and Wiser
(McManus), 24
iPad tablet computer, 9, 24
I-pointer (cursor) in text
document, 116, 117
ISP (Internet Service Provider), 143–144,
145–147, 172

J

Java and JavaScript, 295
jewel box for CD, defined, 224
JPG or JPEG file type, 295
jump list, 59
Junk folder, email, 176
junk or spam email, 180–181, 296

K

keyboard
shortcuts list, 137
standard, 27–32
system tray icon for changing
language, 55
virtual, 32–33, 54
Keyboard language in Charms menu
Settings, 46–47
kilobyte (KB), defined, 295

L

language, changing keyboard,
46–47, 55
laptop computer type, 9, 27, 96
left-click actions from mouse, 24
Libraries, 77, 78–79
license, program, 226

lines, selecting multiple text, 122
LinkedIn, 289
links, web page, 193
Live Mail. *See* email
Live Tile, 41, 213
Livedrive, 164
Lock screen, 19, 37–38, 90

M

Mail app, 173–181
main window, defined, 70
malware, 156–158, 295
maps, searching online, 245
Maps app, 108–112
maximise button in Desktop, 65
McManus, Sean (author)
iPad for the Older and Wiser, 24
*Social Networking for the Older and
Wiser,* 287
Media Center, 276
megabyte (MB), defined, 295
memory, computer, 76
menus
Charms, 34, 43–47
context-sensitive (right-click), 25
dropdown type, 120–121, 294
Internet Explorer, 193–194, 194–195
Start screen options, 112
messages. *See* email
Microsoft Surface tablet computer, 9
minimise button in Desktop, 65
mobile phone technology for Internet
connection, 10
mouse, working with, 24–26
mouse pointer, 24, 98, 117
movies, watching, 276, 281–282
MP3 file type, 295
MSN (Microsoft Network), 295

multitasking, Desktop organising, 59–60
music
    copying files to or from CD, 274–276
    downloading from Spotify, 278–280
    playing, 273, 276–278
    playlist, creating, 276
    Shuffle feature, 277
Music app, 276–278
My Location in Maps, 108–109

N

naming files and folders, 79, 83
Narrator function, Ease of access, 94
navigation buttons
    Internet Explorer, 192
    in windows, 68
netbook computer type, 9
Network in Charms menu Settings,
    45–46
networking of computers
    HomeGroup, 68, 94
    Network in Charms menu Settings,
        45–46
    Networks information, 166–167
    wireless connection, 10, 45–46, 94,
        146, 165–167, 296
Networks information, 166–167
News & Weather category, Windows
    Store, 207–208
Notifications in Charms menu
    Settings, 46
Notifications section, PC Settings, 91

O

online, defined, 145, 296. *See also*
    Internet
Open Office application, 229
Outbox, email, 173, 175–176

P

Paint app, 104–107
paragraph, selecting entire, 122
password
    Internet connection, 150–151
    Lock screen, 38
    multiple passwords, 162
    starting Windows 8, 19
    user accounts, 90
    wireless encryption, 165
PC Settings
    Devices section, 94
    Ease of access section, 94
    General section, 92–93
    HomeGroup section, 94
    Notifications section, 91
    opening, 89
    Personalize section, 90, 91
    Privacy section, 93–94
    Search section, 91
    Share section, 92
    Sync your settings section, 94
    Users section, 90
    Windows update, 95
    Wireless section, 94
PCWisdom website resource, 219
People app, 213–217
peripherals, defined, 18
personal records, protecting, 162
Personalize option for Desktop, 56
Personalize section, PC Settings, 90, 91
phishing scheme, 159–160
Photoshop Elements, installing, 224–228
Picasa application, 230–231, 282–283
pinching and stretching gestures, 23, 27
piracy, software, 228
pixel, defined, 296
playlist, creating, 276
Power in Charms menu Settings, 46
power settings, 96

power symbol, 18
printer, 10, 11
privacy, computer, 288. *See also* security
Privacy section, PC Settings, 93–94
product key for software, location of, 226–227, 228
program, defined, 22, 296. *See also* applications; apps
protecting yourself online
   backing up your data/files, 162–165
   financial transactions, 8, 159–162, 252–253
   firewall, 167
   identity theft, 8, 156
   introduction, 155–156
   Lock screen, 19, 37–38, 90
   malware, 156–158
   passwords (*See* password)
   personal records, 162
   resetting your computer, 93
   spam or junk email, 176, 180–181
   Wi-Fi issues, 165–167

Q

quarantine of computer virus, 157
Quick Access bar, 122–123
Quicklaunch bar, 65

R

radio, listening via Internet, 280
rail tickets, booking online, 266–269
receiving and reading email messages, 179–180, 185
Recycle bin, 53–54
Redo and Undo icons, 124
Refresh button in Internet Explorer, 198
Refresh options, PC Settings, 93
registering with website, 257

removing. *See* deleting
renaming files and folders, 79, 83
replying to email messages, 181
Reset option, PC Settings, 93
Return (Enter) key, 28
ribbon tabs in windows, 66
right-clicking with mouse, 25
ripping (copying) music tracks from CD, 274–275
router, defined, 146, 296

S

SatNav technology, 108
Save As command, 85, 127
saving
   drawings in Paint, 107
   files, 80, 83–85, 164–165
   text document, 125–128
scroll wheel on mouse, 25
scrollbar, Internet Explorer, 195
Search box, 68, 241
search engines
   alternatives to Google, 111, 247
   defined, 237, 296
   Google, 238–247
   introduction, 237–238
   as shopping tool, 253
Search in Charms menu, 44
Search section, PC Settings, 91
searching
   from Desktop interface, 96–97
   for files on your computer, 128
   Help facility, 132
   map information, 111–112, 245
   from Start screen, 47–48, 97–98
security, computer
   backing up your data/files, 162–165
   financial transactions, 8, 159–162, 252–253
   firewall, 167

identity theft, 8, 156
introduction, 155–156
Lock screen, 19, 37–38, 90
malware, 156–158
passwords (*See* password)
personal records, 162
resetting your computer, 93
spam or junk email, 176, 180–181
Wi-Fi issues, 165–167
selecting text, 117–118, 121–122
sending email, 176–180, 184–185
Sent items folder, email, 175
server, defined, 4, 189
Settings in Charms menu, 45–47
Share in Charms menu, 44–45
Share section, PC Settings, 92
shareware software type, 230
sharing computers on a network
HomeGroup, 68, 94
Network in Charms menu
Settings, 45–46
Networks information, 166–167
wireless connection, 10, 45–46, 94,
146, 165–167, 296
Shift keys, 30
shopping on the Internet, 11, 159–162,
251–258
Shuffle feature for playing audio, 277
shutting down computer, 34, 138
side bar, window, 68–69
size limits on email file
attachments, 180
sizing
maps, 109
tiles on Start screen, 40–41, 212–213
windows on Desktop, 65
SkyDrive, 164
Sleep mode, 96
slide show, viewing photo, 282–283
'snailmail,' 145
social networking, 214, 287–290

Social Networking for the Older and Wiser (McManus), 287
software, defined, 229, 296. *See also* applications; apps
Solitaire app, 102–103
Sort By option for Desktop icons, 56
sound, system tray icon, 55
Sound in Charms menu Settings, 46
spam or junk email, 176, 180–181, 296
speed of Internet connection, 147–148
spellchecker in email application,
177–178
Spotify, downloading music from,
278–280
spyware, defined, 296
standard keyboard, 27–32
Start in Charms menu, 45
Start screen
apps compared to applications, 21–22
Charms menu, 34, 43–47
closing apps, 43, 103–104
configuring, 90
displaying all open apps, 42, 218
free compared to paid apps, 211–212
getting started, 19–20
as home for apps, 21
Internet Explorer, 196–199
introduction, 101
Lock screen, 37–38
Mail, 173–181
Maps, 108–112
menu options, 112
moving between apps in, 112,
217–218
Music, 276–278
opening apps, 41, 102–103
Paint, 104–107
People, 213–217
pinning an app to, 198
removing/unpinning apps, 40,
212–213
searching from, 47–48, 97–98

Start screen *(continued)*
    thumbnail images on, 42
    tiles on, 20, 38–41, 212–213
    Windows Store as apps source,
        205–212
Store, 205–212
stretching and pinching gestures, 23, 27
Surface tablet computer, 9
swiping on touch screen, defined, 23
Sync button in email application, 179
Sync your settings section,
        PC Settings, 94
system tray icons, 54–56

T

Tab key, 28–29, 257
tablet computer type, 9
tabs
    Internet Explorer, 193
    ribbon, 66
tap-and-hold gesture on touch screen,
    defined, 23
tapping touch screen to initiate action,
    defined, 23
Task Manager, 135–137
taskbar on Desktop, 54, 58
telephone connection to Internet, 146
text documents, working in
    deleting text, 122, 124–125
    dropdown menus, 120–121
    finding files, 128
    fonts, changing, 118–119, 120
    formatting text, 118–119
    inserting text, 122
    Microsoft Word, compared to, 224
    opening, 115–117
    Quick Access bar, 122–123
    saving, 125–128
    selecting text, 117–118, 121–122

Undo and Redo icons, 124
The Internet for the Older and Wiser
    (Arnold), 283
thumbnail image of app on Start
    screen, 42
ticketless airline booking, 262–266
tiles on Start screen, 20, 38–41,
    78–79, 212–213
time and date, system tray icon, 55–56
title bar on windows, 64
toolbars, 66, 67, 79, 191, 296
tools button, Internet Explorer app, 198
Touch keyboard, PC Settings, 93
touchscreen commands, 22–24
trackball, 24
trackpad, 26–27
traffic information in Maps, 110
train travel, booking online, 266–269
Trainline, booking rail tickets, 266–269
travel, booking online, 6, 261–269
trial versions of software, 230
Trojans (malware), 158, 296
trolling, online, defined, 289
turning computer off, 33–34, 138
turning computer on, 18–19
TV player, 280–281
tweet, defined, 289
Twitter, 289

U

Undo and Redo icons, 124
uninstalling applications, 40
URL (Uniform Resource Locator),
    defined, 192
USB port, defined, 296
USB stick drive, 163
user account, password for, 90
username, Internet connection, 150
Users section, PC Settings, 90

V

video, playing, 276
video search (YouTube), 243–244
virtual keyboard, 32–33, 54
virus, computer, 156–158, 296
volume control, 46, 55

W

web browser
 defined, 294
 Internet Explorer app,
  196–199
 Internet Explorer application
  (Desktop), 78–79, 190–196
 introduction, 189–190
web server, defined, 4, 189
web-based email accounts, 182
wheel on mouse, uses for, 25
whole document, selecting all
  text in, 122
Wi-Fi (wireless) connection to
  Internet, 10, 45–46, 94,
  146, 165–167, 296
Windows 8
 age considerations, 1–3
 beginner's fears, 6–8
 controlling the computer, 22–33
 customising, 89–98
 Desktop (See Desktop interface)
 equipment needed, 8–12
 file system (See files)
 guardian angels, 3
 installing software, 223–233
 Internet uses (See Internet)
 mental approach to computer use, 3
 Start screen (See Start screen)
 turning computer off, 33–34, 138
 turning computer on, 18–19

uses for home computer, 3–4
Windows Explorer, 78–79
Windows Help facility, 133–135
windows in Desktop interface
 breadcrumb bar, 67
 Help button, 67
 main window, defined, 70
 navigation buttons, 68
 opening, 69–70
 Quicklaunch bar, 65
 ribbon, 66–67
 Search box, 68
 side bar, 68–69
 sizing buttons, 65
 structure of, 64
 title bar, 64
 viewing folders, 66
Windows key, 28
Windows Live Essentials, 173, 233
Windows Live Mail. See email
Windows Media Player, 274, 276
Windows Store, 205–212
Windows update, 95
wired connection to Internet, 10
wireless (Wi-Fi) connection to
  Internet, 10, 45–46, 94,
  146, 165–167, 296
Wireless section, PC Settings, 94
word, selecting single, 122
WordPad application
 deleting text, 122, 124–125
 dropdown menus, 120–121
 finding files, 128
 formatting text, 118–119
 inserting text, 122
 Microsoft Word, compared to, 224
 opening, 115–117
 Quick Access bar, 122–123
 saving a document, 125–128
 selecting text, 117–118, 121–122
 Undo and Redo icons, 124

World Wide Web (WWW), 4, 144,
    189–190, 296. *See also* Internet
worm, defined, 296
WPA2 wireless encryption, 165

Y

Yahoo! search engine, 247
YouTube, 243–244

Z

zooming in Maps, 109